Ordinary Mysticism

D<small>ENNIS</small> T<small>AMBURELLO</small>, O.F.M.

PAULIST PRESS
New York/Mahwah, N.J.

Cover design by Christine Taylor.

Library of Congress Cataloging-in-Publication Data

Tamburello, Dennis, 1953-
   Ordinary mysticism / by Dennis Tamburello, OFM.
     p.   cm.
   Includes bibliographical references.
   ISBN 0-8091-3634-1 (alk. paper)
   1. Mysticism. 2. Mysticism—History—Middle Ages, 600-1500. 3. Spirituality. I. Title.
BV5082.2.T36 1996   95-26173
248.2′2—dc20   CIP

Published by Paulist Press
997 Macarthur Boulevard
Mahwah, NJ 07430

Printed and bound in the
United States of America

Contents

Dedicated to the memory of
my father
Anthony C. Tamburello
(1923–1995)

Acknowledgments

The Scripture quotations contained herein are from the New Revised Standard Version Common Bible, copyright 1989 by the Division of Christian Education of the National Council of Churches of Christ in the USA. Used by permission. All rights reserved.

The Publisher gratefully acknowledges use of the following materials: excerpts from the following titles from the Classics of Western Spirituality Series: Bonaventure, *The Soul's Journey into God*; *The Tree of Life*; *The Life of St. Francis*, translated by Ewert Cousins, copyright © 1988; Francis and Clare, *The Complete Works*, translated by Armstrong and Brady, copyright © 1982; Julian of Norwich, *Showings*, translated by Colledge and Walsh, copyright © 1978; Meister Eckhart, *The Essential Sermons, Commentaries, Treatises, and Defense*, translated by Colledge and McGinn, copyright © 1981; Meister Eckhart, *Teacher and Preacher*, edited by Bernard McGinn, copyright © 1986; Teresa of Avila, *The Interior Castle*, translated by Kavanaugh and Rodriguez, copyright © 1979; *The Theologia Germanica of Martin Luther*, translated by Bengt Hoffman, copyright © 1980; all published by Paulist Press. The Publisher also acknowledges the following: Bernard of Clairvaux, *On Loving God*, with an analytical commentary by Emero Stiegman, Cistercian Fathers Series, No. 13B, Kalamazoo, MI: Cistercian Publications, copyright © 1995. A new edition of the translation cited in this book: Bernard of Clairvaux, Treatises III: *On Grace and Free Choice*; *In Praise of the New Knighthood*, translated by Daniel O'Donovan and Conrad Greenia, Cistercian Fathers Series, No. 19. Kalamazoo, MI: Cistercian Publications, copyright © 1977.

Introduction

What does the word "mysticism" mean to most of us? Probably nothing more than a term to describe some of the unusual aspects of Christian belief and practice, things like visions of Christ and Mary, as well as special gifts of grace like the stigmata. Whatever we may think about the importance of such phenomena, they seem far removed from our everyday experience. If this is what we mean by mysticism, it is easy for us to conclude that while there may have been some great mystics in the past we are unlikely to meet one today. Dennis Tamburello's direct and thought-provoking book, *Ordinary Mysticism*, suggests just the opposite: There may well be mystics all around us!

To those who are convinced that mysticism is an exotic, superfluous, perhaps even slightly suspect aspect of our belief, Tamburello's book offers a challenge that cannot be avoided. In clear and engaging language, though without ever sacrificing theological precision, he lays out the practical relevance of mysticism on the basis of the teaching of classic Christian mystics of the medieval and early modern periods, that is, from the twelfth through the sixteenth centuries. *Ordinary Mysticism* shows why the mystical element in Christian faith should be an important aspect of the lives of all who aspire to follow the gospel.

Dennis Tamburello's argument, following the teaching

of the greatest of Christian mystics, shows that the core of mysticism does not consist in ecstatic experiences, unusual visions, miraculous powers, and psychosomatic gifts like the stigmata (though *some* mystics have indeed enjoyed these). Rather, mysticism, or perhaps better what we can call the mystical element in Christianity, consists in finding God's presence in our lives in a more intimate way. Intimacy with God, as a specific and more intense experience of the grace that is the foundation of all Christian living, is what mysticism is all about. Thus every believer should at least desire to be a mystic, and everyone who has experienced some particular moments of such intimacy has shared in what great mystics like Bernard of Clairvaux, Francis of Assisi and Teresa of Avila have enjoyed in a far more intense way.

From this perspective, *Ordinary Mysticism* successfully demonstrates the necessary connection between mysticism and other key aspects of our everyday belief and practice. Far from being another and different way to God open to only a special few, mysticism is open to all because it is always based on God's self-communication to us through Christ and the church. Nor is mysticism to be thought of as a retreat from our active obligations into a purely private sphere of prayer and contemplation. Rather, the mystics have always insisted that true mystical piety is a higher integration of both action and contemplation, that is, of both love of God and love of neighbor. Finally, the mystical life is a life of ever-deepening conversion fueled by the recognition, which few have sensed as strongly as the mystics, that the wonderful mystery of God can never be exhausted by any finite creature. Meister Eckhart, one of the medieval figures often cited in *Ordinary Mysticism*, put it this way in commenting on the passage from the Book of Sirach, "They that eat me, shall yet hunger" (Sir 24:29):

God, as infinite Truth and Goodness and infinite Existence, is the meat of everything that is, that is true, and that is good. And he is hungered for. They feed on him, because they exist, are true, and are good; they hunger, because he is infinite.

Ordinary Mysticism is especially helpful in showing how the teaching of the mystics and a commitment to seeking a more intimate relation to God in our daily lives enriches our understanding of God. Mystical teachers have been in the forefront of those who have challenged stereotyped images of God. This is evident in the ways in which mystics like Julian of Norwich have used feminine language about God as Mother in order to highlight the maternal love of the One who lies beyond all sexual division. It is equally evident in the negative mystics, like Eckhart and his pupil John Tauler, who insistently remind us that God lies beyond not only sexual distinction, but also beyond all human language and conception—hidden in the "dazzling darkness" of supreme mystery.

Ordinary Mysticism is timely in this ecumenical age by underlining the fact that mysticism is the common heritage of all Christians, whatever their denominational affiliation. Dennis Tamburello aptly refers to John Calvin's "mystical sensitivity." Other great leaders of Protestantism, Martin Luther and John Wesley to name but two, while not exactly mystics in the full-fledged sense of Teresa of Avila and others, were deeply touched by the mystical element in Christianity. We must also remember that all Christian mysticism rests on the foundations constructed by the Fathers of Eastern Christianity, whose teaching continues to burn brightly in the Orthodox Churches throughout the world.

To be a Christian is to be called to seek for a more intimate, that is, a mystical experience of God. And, as Bernard of Clairvaux once said, "It is God alone who can never be sought in vain, even when he cannot be found."

Bernard McGinn
Divinity School
University of Chicago

Preface

This book originated as a lecture delivered in May 1985 at Calvert House, the Catholic Student Center at the University of Chicago. I had been a student of the mystics for four years at the Divinity School of that university. In my survey of Christian mystical texts, I often encountered the strange and exotic language and concepts that have led many people to abandon the mystics as hopelessly impossible to comprehend or appreciate. Indeed, in the year-long graduate seminar that introduced me to the mystics, the discussions were sometimes incredibly abstract, high-level theologizing that would bore the average person to death. I think even the flies on the wall may have fled the room at times.

While this "academic" approach to the mystics taught me some important things, it did not address something else that so often happened to me when I read them. That something was **inspiration**. I found the mystics, even the ones who lived centuries ago, to be a gold mine for contemporary spirituality. So one day, I sat down for a brainstorming session in which I asked myself: "What do the mystics say to me *personally*?"

My answer to this question formed the outline of that first lecture on mysticism given at Calvert House. The lecture was later expanded to a day-long workshop, and finally a week-long mini-course that was given at St. Francis of Assisi Parish in Brant Beach, N.J., in August 1987. It has subsequently been given in several other settings, before both Catholic and Protestant audiences. I am grateful to several people for encouraging me to expand these materials into a book, especially Gregory Zoltowski, Rev. Chris Aridas, and Robert Heller.

It is my hope that this book will help people in their spiritual journey. It is not a book written for scholars. Some of my colleagues in the academic world will undoubtedly be disappointed that it does not attempt to break any new scholarly ground. Its purpose is more modest: to share with interested Christians the fruits of one person's academic and personal reflection on the Christian mystical tradition. The book therefore does not presuppose any formal study of theology on the part of the reader.

It bears repeating that this book represents one person's attempt to understand the practical relevance of the mystics. I do not claim authoritative status for these reflections. Indeed, the mystics would be the first to disown me if I did! They knew as well as anyone that God is mystery, and that that mystery can never be fully fathomed by any human being. If these essays inspire the reader to look further into the writings of the mystics, or even simply to appreciate them not as mere navel-gazers but as men and women deeply engrossed in the mysteries of life, then this book will have served its purpose.

One of the editorial decisions I made was to include notes in the book. These notes direct the reader to the exact location of the quoted sources, and they also occasionally expand upon topics that are related to the chapter but may not be of interest to all readers. For example, some notes give additional historical or theological information on issues that have been controversial, but would distract from the main argument if placed directly in the text. Readers should feel free to consult the notes or disregard them.

No book is produced in isolation, and this one especially is the product of many hands, directly and indirectly. I wish to thank my professors at the University of Chicago, especially Brian A. Gerrish, Bernard McGinn, and Jerald Brauer, who guided me through a dissertation on Calvin and mysticism that was later published as *Union with Christ* by Westminster/John Knox Press. Some of what I learned from that project appears in a somewhat different form in the present volume. Bernard McGinn deserves a special word of thanks for introducing me to the study of mysticism through his Mysticism and Theology seminar in 1982–83. In addition, I am grateful to all those who have participated in the lectures and workshops on which this book is based. Their comments and suggestions have been invaluable.

Several people deserve a special word of thanks for reading through portions of the manuscript and offering comments on both style and content. These include Eileen Girten, Sharon Heuschele, Joyce Gizzarelli, Joe Makowiec, Matthew Scarchilli, Fr. Jacob Parappally, M.S.F.S., Fr. Augustinus Wehrmeier, O.F.M., and my students in the Mysticism Seminar at Siena College in Spring 1993 and Fall 1995.

Finally, I wish to thank the Franciscans of Holy Name Province, who have encouraged and supported my academic endeavors, my colleagues and students at Siena College who have afforded me a wonderful environment in which to teach, and my family, who up to now have told me that they never understand anything that I write. I hope this book will be different.

On July 23, 1995, after this work had gone into production, my beloved father, Anthony C. Tamburello, passed from this world to the next. I dedicate this book to his memory, with love to my mother, brother, and sisters.

1

What Is Mysticism?

There is an old Peanuts cartoon in which Charlie Brown's sister Sally is writing an essay on "Church History." She begins by writing, appropriately enough: "To talk about church history, we have to begin at the beginning." After a pause, she continues: "Our pastor was born in 1930."

Since becoming a historian of Christian theology, I have always wondered how people can so easily forget that the Christian church has had a history that extends back centuries before they (or their pastors!) were born. There is a strong tendency for people to identify tradition with "the way the church was while I was growing up." Thus, many Christians seem to have little interest in looking into the more distant past. They are content to leave this to the theologians and the historians. As for themselves, they are more interested in what is going on in the church *now*, or at least what has taken place within the memory of their lifetimes.

This apparent non-interest in getting a full picture of their history leaves Christians at a great loss. The heritage of Christianity is long and rich—and one does not have to be a professional theologian or historian to tap it. Indeed, to someone who asks: "What could people who lived several hundred years ago possibly have to say to us—we who live in the late twentieth century in such a highly complex society?" the Christian historian might answer: "Come and see (Jn 1:39); you might be surprised!"

I must admit that I was pretty surprised myself at first. When I first started reading the works of mystics from earlier centuries, my interest was purely academic. I was not expecting to find much of value for my own life. I preferred to read contemporary authors like Henri Nouwen for my own spiritual enrichment. To my great amazement, I discovered that periods like the so-called middle ages offer more insights that relate to contemporary spirituality than I ever thought possible. Indeed, I learned that my own modern spiritual heroes were themselves drawing constantly from this rich font of tradition, not concocting a totally new spirituality.

Unfortunately, in our age the word "medieval" has taken on a negative connotation. In Christian circles, for example, one sometimes hears the phrase, "Get out of the middle ages." Medieval has come to mean "outdated" or "passé." This impression seems to be confirmed when one first reads medieval literature, most of which is not easy to warm up to. But when one takes the time to grapple with it, one begins to see that much of it has enormous relevance for our time.

The goal of this book is to introduce the reader to a number of themes that were especially (but not exclusively) prominent in the twelfth through the sixteenth centuries, an exceedingly fertile period in the history of Christian mysticism. Christian historians see this as the time when mysticism came to full bloom in Christianity, when earlier trends and experiences converged in a most creative and integrative way.

This book, then, will focus on the mysticism of the so-called "late middle ages," in order to keep these reflections within reasonable bounds. The book is intended to function as a sampler and a primer. It does not pretend to deal with every conceivable theme from medieval mysticism that has relevance to contemporary spirituality. Indeed, my principal hope for this book is that it will inspire readers to delve more deeply into the writings of the mystics and to find other insights that will enhance their spirituality.

Toward a Definition of Mysticism

Before going any further, it is important to define the terms of our discussion. "Mysticism" is quite an elusive term, which means many different things to different people. The *New Catholic Encyclopedia* appropriately begins its article on mysticism by describing it as "a term used to cover a literally bewildering variety of states of mind."[1] It has been used in a generic sense to refer to almost any kind of religious experience, and in a very specific sense to refer to particular kinds of exotic religious experience, such as ecstasies, visions, trances, an experience of being outside of one's body, etc. Most people who are familiar with the term at all tend to understand it in the second sense: as strange or exotic religious experiences that are enjoyed by an elite few, and an eccentric and bizarre few at that!

Given this popular view of mysticism as something spooky and strange, the reader can probably appreciate one cynic's definition of mysticism as "beginning in mist (myst-), centering in an 'I' (-i-), and ending in schism (-cism)." In other words, mystics are first of all in a fog, people who are riding on "cloud nine" or gazing for hours each day at their navels. Secondly, mystics are self-centered, totally preoccupied with their personal, individual experiences of the sacred. Finally, since their religion is so highly personal, they end up seceding from the community of faith and becoming opponents of institutional religion.

I do not know exactly where this definition came from, but it is an excellent example of how much mysticism has been misunderstood. The mystics who will be discussed in this book do not fit any part of this definition. Evelyn Underhill, one of the great scholars of mysticism in our century, makes a remark that is relevant in this regard: "Those mystics, properly speaking, can only be studied in their works: works which are for the most part left unread by those who now talk much about mysticism."[2]

Numerous books and articles about mysticism are guilty of Underhill's charge. They make sweeping judgments against mysticism, none of which can be substantiated in the writings of the mystics themselves. The reasons for this prejudice against mysticism are many, and there is no need to go into them here.[3] Let us simply attempt to work toward a definition in which the people we refer to as mystics might be able to recognize themselves.

The origin of the word "mysticism" is found in the Greek word *mustikos*, which is derived from *mustes*, "one initiated into secret rites." This in turn is derived from *muein*, "to close the eyes or mouth, hence to keep secret (as in religious initiation)."[4] Thus, "mystical" can have the connotation of "mysterious" or "secret." This etymology certainly squares with many people's perception of mysticism as an esoteric encounter with the mysterious (or the sacred, or God) to which few human beings have access. However, as we shall see, mysticism does not have to be defined as a phenomenon that is only enjoyed by an elite few.

Narrow and Broad Definitions

Most definitions of mysticism that are proposed by Christian theologians[5] consistently mention certain characteristics. The focus in such definitions is usually on the subjective ("felt") experience of being in an intimate relationship with God. This intimate relationship has been described in a number of different ways, including "direct contemplation or vision of God, rapture or ecstasy, deification, living in Christ, the birth of the Word in the soul, radical obedience to the directly-present will of God, and especially union with God."[6]

This list by Bernard McGinn says "especially" union with God because the category of union has been prominent at least since the twelfth century, and even today people characteristically think of mysticism in terms of an experience of union with God. In fact, in her classic work on mysticism, Evelyn Underhill defined mysticism as follows: "Mysticism, in its pure form, is...the science of union with the Absolute, and nothing else, and...the mystic is the person who attains to this union, not the person who talks about it."[7]

However, there are broader definitions than this. Theologian Ernst Troeltsch states: "In the widest sense of the word, mysticism is simply the insistence upon a direct inward and present religious experience."[8] This kind of definition looks upon mysticism as being, in its basic form, a dimension of all religious piety, rather than as an "esoteric" phenomenon that can only be enjoyed by specially gifted or eccentric individuals.

This brings us to what is, for our purposes, the crucial question: **Is mysticism something to be enjoyed by a select few, or is there something in it for everybody?** The thesis of this book is that there is a sense in which mysti-

cism can be a part of every Christian's life, without denying that some Christians have had a more intense kind of
mystical experience.

Karl Rahner, arguably the premier Roman Catholic theologian of the twentieth century, wrote an essay that is
very helpful in this connection.[9] Rahner rejects any understanding of Christian mysticism that speaks of a special
grace given to a few. For him, there can be no such thing
as an intermediate state between the "ordinary" experience of grace (i.e., experiencing God in our present existence) and the experience of eternal glory. When Rahner
speaks of grace, he generally means the presence or self-
communication of God. God is equally present to all
human beings, so there can be no "mystical" grace as
opposed to "ordinary" grace. Thus Rahner avoids speaking
of a mystical elite.

How, then, does Rahner account for the fact that some
people do claim to have had an extraordinary experience
of intimacy with God, which they describe in strange or
exotic terms? Rahner will say that mystical experience is a
specific mode of the ordinary experience of grace. In
other words, some people experience the grace that is
equally available to all "to an existentially intensive
degree."[10] Such an experience is not essential to a full
Christian life, nor to salvation. Rahner is therefore comfortable with saying that "mysticism is not necessarily a
part of every Christian life."[11] All have experienced grace;
not all are mystics.

With all due respect to Karl Rahner, it is not necessary
to exclude ordinary Christians from mystical experience.[12]
Rahner is correct in his assertion that mystics do not
receive a special or better kind of grace; but by defining
mysticism only in terms of existentially intense experiences
(which in itself can mean a number of different things, as

Rahner himself admits), he denies that there can be a more ordinary type of mysticism that is accessible to all, such as Troeltsch's definition suggests.

One way of resolving this tension is to adopt a distinction such as the following. Let us use the term "mysticism" (with a lower-case "m") to refer to the experience of God's presence (and the response to that presence) that all religious persons enjoy to a greater or lesser degree. In turn, let us use "Mysticism" (with a capital "M") to refer to those more extraordinary or intense experiences of grace: a sense of being outside one's own body, a vision or ecstasy, an experience of pure contemplation, etc. The goal of this book, then, is to show how some of the extraordinary *Mystics* of our tradition can speak to us more ordinary *mystics* who live in the late twentieth century.

Mysticism: One Element of Religion

Perhaps the best explanation of ordinary mysticism has been offered by Friedrich von Hügel, a theologian from the early twentieth century, in his book *The Mystical Element of Religion*. Von Hügel is especially helpful because he situates mysticism in relation to other elements of the Christian life. Properly understood, mysticism is not the only thing that Christianity is about, but is only one of several dimensions of a life of faith. Von Hügel is well aware that the mystics have often been accused of ignoring the other dimensions.

Von Hügel sees three elements that are always and everywhere present in religion. He calls the first element the institutional, although "organizational" might be a better word. This element embraces the external aspects of religion: authority, history, tradition, and the like. "Religion is here, above all," he says, "a fact and a thing."

This is what most of us often equate with religion: the church buildings and people that we can see, the creeds that we profess, etc.

The second element is the speculative, which according to von Hügel would embrace the "reasoning, argumentative, abstractive side of human nature....Religion here becomes Thought, System, a Philosophy." This element of religion is operative whenever we try to make sense of or talk about our faith. Most of us do this informally; there are also theologians who do it professionally (sometimes unfortunately in a way that confounds people who don't have Ph.D.s in theology).

Von Hügel characterizes the third element of religion as the experimental (read: "experiential") and mystical. "Here religion is rather felt than seen or reasoned about, is loved and lived rather than analyzed, is action and power, rather than either external fact or intellectual verification."[13]

Von Hügel insists that, in a proper approach to religion, none of these elements ever stands totally apart from the others. Indeed, he believes that when people stress one element while attempting to eliminate or suppress one or both of the others, they only cause themselves problems. I think von Hügel is absolutely right about this. Let us look at some examples to illustrate the point.

The Institutional Element

We all know religious people who are absolutely loyal to the external trappings of a particular organized religion. These persons tend to live totally out of what von Hügel would call the institutional element. Such people are often very narrow and exclusive in their thinking. Their religion seems to claim their total allegiance, to the point that knowledge and insight from other sources (e.g., other academic disciplines, or even personal experiences that do not fit in with their own rigid beliefs) will be either ignored or rejected as worthless. These people see their religion as "fixed in itself, as given once for all, and to be defended against all change and interpretation."[14] Anyone who has a different perspective, or who does not follow the "party line" on every last detail pertaining to the institution, is assumed to be a dangerous subversive, or even under the influence of Satan. Probably we have all met people who fit these descriptions, like biblical fundamentalists whose narrow understanding of Christian beliefs is absolutely unshakable (and who would never accept that there could be other legitimate interpretations of the bible),[15] or ultra-conservative dogmatists, of whatever religious denomination, who see their church as a fixed entity that can never change or adapt to a new situation. Sharing the facts of history with them, showing them that church history has never been anything but a dynamic process with a lot of changes and ups and downs, never seems to do any good.

The problems with this narrow approach to religion are obvious. It is legalistic, intolerant, and naively uncritical of institutions. Both the church and other institutions often tend to be divinized in this kind of perspective.[16] This is why political and religious arch-conservatism often go hand in hand. "Holy Mother Church" and "Uncle Sam" are always right, and "error has no rights." Believers who fit this description are sometimes willing to bully other Christians into submission to the institution at all costs, even at the cost of violating their own consciences. There is no room for dissent, or even for questions. Von Hügel would say that this kind of exclusive, repressive approach to religion is institutionalism run amok. In its worst manifestations it does not even deserve to be called Christianity.

On the opposite extreme are those people who would eliminate any institutional element in religion. Religion becomes a purely personal matter, a relationship between "me and God." This is certainly a strong tendency for Americans, who as a society have come to the point of exalting the individual at the expense of the common good.[17] Individualism (religious and otherwise), it need hardly be pointed out, is a very attractive option, especially to young people. Why be bound by what other people, or formal organizations, say, when one can just do what one likes, make one's own rules? The problem, of course, is that we don't need to look very far to see the bitter fruits of this kind of approach to life, the approach that says "I am not going to let anybody tell me what to do," or that makes wisdom something to be pursued in isolation from others. The alienation and brokenness that exist in our society, due in part to this pervasive social attitude, speak for themselves.

But individualism is even more problematic from a religious perspective. Indeed, the phrase "privatized Christianity" is simply a contradiction in terms. Such an approach is hardly the one promoted by Jesus, who very clearly called his followers to live, work, and pray *as a community*. As Paul says in 1 Corinthians 12, we are called to be one body. While there certainly is room for an individual relationship with God, the context of that relationship for Christians is one's participation in the body that is the church.

To sum up, both an exclusive stress on institutional religion and a total denial of institutional religion are imbalanced approaches that a Christian should avoid. Similarly, problems arise when one takes either an exclusively intellectual or, conversely, an anti-intellectual approach.

The Intellectual Element

There are certainly people for whom religion is a purely intellectual thing. In the academic world, one often meets people who have a strong interest in the study of religion, but who are clearly uninterested in faith as a personal commitment to be lived out in everyday action and celebrated in worship.[18] This kind of inconsistency is nothing new. Consider the ancient Corinthians, whom Paul found to be intensely interested in arguments about religion; but when it came time to put their Christianity into practice, it was a different story. All kinds of immorality and uncharitable behavior prevailed, which Paul spent most of his first letter to the Corinthians addressing.

Many Christians *profess* to be interested in all aspects of their faith, but in fact they are stuck in the argumentation mode. This is an occupational hazard for professional theologians, who can easily expend all of their energy weaving elaborate theories, and never leave their ivory towers long enough to deal with real people and real issues. As time goes on, this isolation takes a toll on their theology, making it less and less relevant to the complex world in which they live.

Francis of Assisi, who always had a suspicion about having too much formal education (because it could make one proud and "extinguish the spirit of prayer and devotion"), made some incisive remarks about the difference between talking about imitating Jesus and actually doing so:

> Let all of us, brothers, look to the Good Shepherd Who suffered the passion of the cross to save His sheep. The sheep of the Lord followed Him in tribulation and persecution, in insult and hunger, in infirmity and temptation, and in everything else, and they have received everlasting life from the Lord because of these things. Therefore, it is a

great shame for us, servants of God, that while the saints [actually] did such things, we wish to receive glory and honor by [merely] recounting their deeds.[19]

To be sure that no one misses the point, Francis goes on to say:

...those religious are killed by the letter who do not wish to follow the spirit of Sacred Scripture, but only wish to know [what] the words [are] and [how to] interpret them to others. And those are given life by the spirit of Sacred Scripture who do not refer to themselves any text which they know or seek to know, but, by word and example, return everything to the most high Lord God to Whom every good belongs.[20]

Of course, theologians are not the only ones who fall into this trap. It can happen to anyone who reduces religion to intellectual arguments rather than facing its challenges.

On the opposite end of the spectrum are the anti-intellectuals, those who seem to want to check their brains at the door of the church as they enter. Such people regard all speculative theology as dangerous, and reject a critical interpretation of the bible as misguided or even satanic. Exclusive institutionalism and anti-intellectualism are often found together (as in some arch-conservative Roman Catholics), but there are also some who are both anti-institutional and anti-intellectual (as in some fundamentalists). Either a narrow understanding of church dogma or a literalistic reading of scripture buttresses the faith of these anti-intellectuals. What they seem to lack most is a sense of history, which clearly shows that both scripture and tradition or dogma did not just come out of a hat, but came to a gradual (and not always unanimous) acceptance in the history of Christianity. For example, there were people who argued against the inclusion of certain books that are now a part of our bible,[21] and "conservatives" back in the fourth century who did not wish to accept the innovative wording of the Nicene Creed, which spoke of Jesus as "one in being with the Father."

What is most disconcerting about the anti-intellectuals is that in the midst of a shallow and sometimes downright misunderstanding of the truths of the faith, they claim to know the truth exactly and fully. Other Christians, more humble in their claims to know the truth, find themselves frustrated when they are unfortunate enough to get dragged into a conversation with these people. It is hard to have a genuine interchange with people who already think they know everything!

A balanced approach to the intellectual element of religion recognizes that we are expected to use God's gift of human reason in reflecting upon and living out our faith. At the same time, it recognizes the limits of human knowing, and accepts that there are mysterious aspects of our faith, that not everything can be figured out.

This approach also recognizes that the intellectual element of religion must be balanced by the others. Thus, it is willing to give serious attention to the common wisdom of the community, including a particular community's dogmatic statements and moral codes, in order to avoid a kind of privatized intellectualism. In other words, a balanced intellectual approach to Christianity (or any religion, for that matter) leaves room for the institutional dimension without allowing it to dominate unduly.

The Mystical Element

Finally we come to the mystical element of religion. Here, too, there is a danger of one-sidedness or extremism. There are many people who are quite emotionally involved with their religion. They may be charismatics or pentecostals, also known as "born-again Christians." They have obviously had a powerful religious experience that has led them to confess Jesus as their personal Lord and Savior with intense fervor and enthusiasm. Their style of prayer is also unique, often being characterized by speaking in tongues (praying in an unintelligible language), long testimonies about God's saving action in their lives, or even fainting (being "slain in the Spirit," as it is called). Other people might not be quite so zealous as the ones just described, but still have a strong emotional or experiential component in their faith, perhaps as a result of an uplifting retreat or an experience like Marriage Encounter or Cursillo.

The resurgence of a strong experiential or mystical component in contemporary Christianity is, however, a mixed blessing. On the one hand, the more mystically-inclined Christians have given a real shot in the arm to their respective churches, which have so often been caught up in exclusive institutionalism or intellectualism. These people have given life to the churches; they have reminded other Christians that their faith is something to be savored and celebrated, that they need to be passionate about their faith and not just go through the motions every Sunday, barely mumbling the prayers and hymns and dozing through the sermons (although the quality of some sermons gives people good reason to doze). Furthermore, these enthusiastic Christians remind their sisters and brothers that religion is not something they should take off the shelf for an hour a week, but something to be lived wholeheartedly each and every day.

On the other hand, an overemphasis on the mystical can create problems. According to von Hügel, persons who overly stress the mystical tend toward self-centeredness and pure emotionalism.[22] People can get caught up in external trappings like speaking in tongues or being slain in the Spirit. For example, there have been charismatic groups where people who do not receive the gift of tongues feel as if there is something wrong with their prayer life, while people with this gift begin to have a superior attitude.

It is interesting to hear what Paul has to say to the Corinthians, who were becoming infatuated with the more exotic gifts of the Spirit like speaking in tongues. According to Paul, all gifts are for the upbuilding of the church, and the greatest gift is love (perhaps precisely because, as Paul describes love, it is *not* self-centered). At one point (1 Cor 14:18), Paul says that he would rather speak five good words of prophecy that will benefit the community than ten thousand words in a tongue.

Von Hügel is convinced that the way to avoid the pitfalls of an excessive mysticism is to keep a balance with the other two elements of religion. Fanatical mysticism tends to shut out both the institutional and intellectual elements. On the other hand, an exclusion of the mystical element is equally odious, as the above descriptions of exclusive institutionalism and intellectualism have shown. Without an openness to the experiential dimension, religion runs the risk of becoming either a rigid, intolerant dogmatism or a cold, analytical word game.

I would suggest that the mystical element of religion is really the most fundamental. The other two elements build on religious experience, as it is reflected upon and lived out in everyday life. This does not mean that mystical awareness always comes first chronologically, or that it occurs in isolation from the other elements. Nevertheless, religion is built fundamentally on an *experience* of God or the sacred. Unfortunately, both religious institutions and religious intellectuals often forget this. Without religious experience, their houses are built on sand.

It is important to note that the mystical dimension of religion embraces more than just a subjective experience of God's presence when we pray. Recall how von Hügel defines the mystical element: "Here religion is rather felt than seen or reasoned about, is loved and lived rather than analyzed, is action and power, rather than either external fact or intellectual verification."[23] Notice that the mystical element includes loving and living, action and power, words that we would associate with Christianity in action. Ideally, then, mysticism is not restricted to personal experiences of God's presence in prayer, but also encompasses our everyday struggle to live out our Christianity.

In a way, von Hügel's understanding of the mystical element of religion is close to what people usually mean by the term "spirituality."[24] One could argue endlessly about the relationship between the two. Are they synonyms? Is mysticism a dimension of spirituality? etc. However, this book will not enter into this argument. The most important point is this: the mystical element of religion, when properly understood, does not shut out the active dimension of Christian life. Indeed, as we shall see, the great mystics of the Christian tradition are almost unanimous in insisting that a life of loving service to others is the fruit of mystical prayer.

The Importance of Balance

After presenting the three elements of religion, von Hügel concedes that it is very tempting to live on the basis of a single element, for "the religious temper longs for simplification." However, the unity for which we long will only be achieved when there is a balance and a harmonization of all three elements in our lives.[25] Thus, it is not surprising to find von Hügel less interested in a unique experience of union with God than in the integration of mysticism with the other dimensions of the religious life. There is a unity *in* multiplicity, which he contrasts with the "impoverishing simplification" of one element's domination.[26] This is why he wants nothing to do with what he calls "Pure Mysticism":

> Is there, then, strictly speaking, such a thing as a specifically distinct, self-sufficing, purely Mystical mode of apprehending Reality? I take it, *distinctly not*; and that all the errors of the Exclusive Mystic proceed precisely from the contention that Mysticism does constitute such an entirely separate, completely self-supported kind of human experience.[27]

Of course, the same is true for pure institutionalism and intellectualism, as the discussion above has tried to show.

"Immediate" Experience of God?

When von Hügel gets down to defining the mystical element of religion more closely, he sounds a lot like Troeltsch.[28] He speaks of the "presence of, and the operative penetration by the Infinite Spirit, within the human spirit," or of "*some*, however implicit, however slight, however intermittent, sense and experience of the Infinite" that is shared by all human beings.[29] In other words, mysticism has to do with a basic awareness of and experience of the sacred that is open to all people.

There is one aspect of these definitions that is problematic from a Christian point of view. Troeltsch speaks of mysticism as a "*direct* inward and present religious experience"; von Hügel speaks of "*penetration* by the Infinite Spirit." Similarly, Rufus Jones defines mysticism as "that type of religion which puts the emphasis on the *immediate* awareness of relation with God, on *direct* and intimate consciousness of the divine presence."[30] Notice the italicized words in these quotations (the italics are added). They imply that in mystical experience, one has an unmediated experience of God. In other words, one can experience God directly, without needing any external helps. It's like the difference between buying something directly from the factory and buying it through a retailer.

But from the very beginning, Christians have believed that the experience of God is always mediated somehow. As Jerald Brauer puts it, *Christian* mysticism "always has some relation to the person of Christ, the reality of the Church, the Christian ethic, and the Christian sacraments."[31] In the history of Christianity, many mystics were criticized, and even condemned, whenever they spoke about an intimacy with God that seemed to bypass the role of Christ, or of scripture, or of the sacraments, or of the church in general.

It is not hard to see why the institutional authorities of the various Christian churches would be threatened by mystics. After all, if people can have a direct experience of God, apart from any "go-betweens," then the institution becomes superfluous. And we know how institutions tend to get caught up with their own importance!

Unfortunately, mystics in general have often gotten a "bad rap" from the institutions of which they were a part. There were, of course, a few mystics who were anti-institutional. But most of them, especially those who will be discussed in this book, were extremely loyal to their churches, and publicly active in roles of Christian service. In many cases, when things the mystics said were formally condemned, the statements were taken out of context and distorted. There are some mystics who only now, centuries after their deaths, are beginning to be appreciated by the Christian churches—people who were once regarded as heretics and subversives and are now recognized to be religious geniuses.[32]

In any case, von Hügel's argument against pure mysticism is important because it highlights what is unique about *Christian* mysticism: that it does *not* bypass Christ, the church, or the sacraments. Rather, mysticism is part of a bigger picture that includes these things.

Still, there is something about an experience of God that does seem direct and unmediated, isn't there? If you've ever had an experience that you call religious, you know what this means. A sense of God's presence just seems to fill you and to surround you, and the experience is so powerful you know that you are not just imagining it.[33] It is wonderful and scary at the same time. How can we account for this without denying that mysticism must have a relationship to the church?

Some authors have suggested a notion of "mediated immediacy"—in other words, we can have a sense of our intimate relationship with God that we *experience* subjectively as immediate, but which in fact is mediated by God's grace. As one author, John Baillie, puts it:

> Though we are more directly and intimately confronted with the presence of God than with any other presence, it does not follow that He is ever present to us *apart* from all other presences. And, in fact, it is the witness of experience that only 'in, with and under' other presences is the divine presence ever vouchsafed to us....Clearly, then, the immediacy of God's presence to our souls is a mediated immediacy.[34]

For Baillie, this apparently self-contradictory phrase only makes sense in light of a "conception of history as something that happens in the present." Baillie speaks of his knowledge of God as first coming to him from his parents and church community. He came to believe that God not only "used these media but that in using them He actually did reveal Himself to *my* soul." Thus he arrived at the conclusion: "God reveals Himself to me only through others who went before, yet in so doing reveals Himself to me now."[35]

Similarly, Bernard Lonergan, one of the great Roman Catholic theologians of our century, asserts that except for infants, who live in a "world of immediacy," there is no experience that we have that is not mediated by meaning. Even in the "prayerful mystic's cloud of unknowing," there is what he calls a "mediated return to immediacy."[36]

It is true that mystics sometimes use language that suggests an unmediated experience of God. But in their defense, it must be noted that mystics, in their attempt to put into words an experience that is virtually indescribable, tend to use language in a paradoxical way. Statements that seem to imply a total immediacy to God are often clearly qualified in other contexts. This is why it is important not to judge a mystic without having a thorough knowledge of what he or she actually said. It is unfortunate that this piece of advice has often gone unheeded in Christian history.

A Medieval Definition of Mysticism

This chapter has attempted to provide a workable general understanding of mysticism and how it relates to other dimensions of Christianity. Von Hügel's schema is not the only one we can use to sort out the relationship, but it is certainly a helpful one. Before moving on to discuss specific contributions of the mystics, let us consider one other definition of mysticism. Given by Jean Gerson (1363–1429), it is a good general description of much of the mysticism of the middle ages:

> Mystical theology is experiential knowledge of God attained through the union of spiritual affection with Him. Through this union the words of the Apostle are fulfilled: "He who clings to God is one spirit with Him (1 Cor 6:17)."[37]

Notice that Gerson refers to mystical theology (i.e., the reflection on mystical experience) as *experiential* knowledge of God. Indeed, for the mystics, to know God is to experience God in a personal way. This is often described in terms of love—to know God is to love God and to know that one is loved by God. The mystics generally know nothing of a purely intellectual knowledge of God.

As noted earlier, in the late middle ages union with God became the preferred way of describing an experience of intimacy with the divine. In fact, Paul's statement from 1 Corinthians about becoming "one spirit with God" was frequently quoted. The terminology is significant, for it implies that a Christian becomes one with God spiritually (usually described as conforming one's will to God's will) rather than "essentially" (i.e., in the sense of losing one's identity and being totally absorbed into God). An essential union implies an elimination of all distinction between God and ourselves—a notion that Christianity has tended to shun.[38]

I think it is fair to say that the goal of most Christian mysticism, both ordinary and extraordinary, is to become "one spirit with God." The medieval mystics have a great deal to offer to contemporary Christians on this topic, but they also have much to say about several other aspects of the Christian life. Each of these aspects will be treated in a separate chapter. They are: (1) images of God, (2) grace and freedom, or God's invitation and our response,

(3) conversion as a lifelong process, and (4) contemplation and action. The final chapter will explore the mystics' views on union with God.

I now invite the reader to journey with me through the writings of the mystics, and to savor their unique insights into the Christian life.

2

The Knowledge of God

Why is the Catholic Church holy?
The Catholic Church is holy because it was founded by
Jesus Christ, who is all holy, and because it teaches, according to the will of Christ, holy doctrines, and provides a
means of leading a holy life, thereby giving holy members
to every age.

Many of us, I suspect, received a decidedly "doctrinal"
upbringing in our faith. This is certainly true of Roman
Catholics who are old enough to remember life before the
Second Vatican Council (a venerable group to which I
myself belong, if barely). Our religious education consisted
mainly of memorizing questions and answers from the so-
called Baltimore Catechism. We studied it before our first
communion, and we studied it again before our confirmation. The catechism gave us the facts that we needed to
know about God and the church in order to be good
Catholics. Similar catechisms exist in many other Christian
communities (e.g., the Lutheran and Presbyterian). Some
are still in use.

Quoted above is a specific question and answer from the
old Baltimore Catechism. It is one that I know by heart to
this day, because in my fifth grade confirmation class, I
was called on to give the answer and suddenly drew a
blank. I was sternly admonished by the pastor—who was

teaching the class personally—to write the answer out five times. I haven't forgotten it since.

For Roman Catholicism and many other Christian communities, it has traditionally been seen as very important for their members to know the truths of the faith. There is a certain value to this, as we noted in Chapter 1 when we discussed von Hügel's intellectual component of religion.

There is, however, also a danger of over-intellectualizing our faith.[1] The great Protestant theologian, John Calvin, once said that to ask the question "What is God?" is to toy with idle speculation. In other words, to want to know about the nature of the Godhead in itself is really not appropriate for a Christian. In his most famous work, *Institutes of the Christian Religion*, Calvin asks:

> What help is it...to know a God with whom we have nothing to do? Rather, our knowledge should serve first to teach us fear and reverence; secondly, with it as our guide and teacher, we should learn to seek every good from him, and, having received it, to credit it to his account.[2]

Thus, Calvin insists that we should only want to know what God has done for us; in line with this, we should recognize God as the fountain of all goodness.[3]

Calvin's teaching on the knowledge of God reflects a mystical theme that was strong in the middle ages: that the experience of God is more important than purely intellectual knowledge. Not that it is a question of one or the other; in fact, it can be said that experience and cognition go hand in hand, as we shall see.

Before we go any further, perhaps a word is in order as to why we are bringing John Calvin into our discussion of mysticism. I have become convinced that it is wrong to think of mysticism as something Catholic as opposed to Protestant. If there is anything that one learns when studying the history of spirituality, it is that there are great spiritual writers in all traditions (including non-Christian ones). It is important, in this day and age, to get beyond labels and to try to understand what we all have in common, without denying that genuine differences remain.

So, we should not dismiss at the outset any Christian writer as having nothing of value to say about mysticism. In Calvin's case particularly, there has been a long history of Protestant writers denying that he had any connection with mysticism. There are many reasons for this, which we need not go into here.[4] Suffice it to say that contrary to most people's general impression of him, Calvin did have a mystical sensitivity. We will occasionally be seeing his name again in the pages that follow.

What we have at our disposal today, in the writings of the mystics, is mystical *theology*: the attempt to articulate in words the meaning of a particular faith-experience. It is important to remember that the *experience* is primary. For most of the classic mystics, to know God is precisely to be in a relationship with God, particularly to experience and give thanks for God's benefits, and to give glory to God by our lives. It is not, as Calvin says, to figure out the essence of God in some way, though many have tried to do that in the history of Christian thought.

Knowledge and Love of God Connected

Bernard of Clairvaux (1090–1153) is one of the great examples of a mystic who stresses the connection between knowledge and love of God. As a young man, Bernard joined the Cistercians, a reform movement within Benedictine monasticism, and later became one of the Order's most famous abbots and statesmen. Let us look at a few of his reflections on this subject.

In one of his many sermons on the Song of Songs, Bernard speaks of those who knew God but refused to honor him.[5] These people, he claims, did not have

> a revelation of the Holy Spirit; for even though they possessed knowledge they did not love....They were content with the knowledge that gives self-importance, but ignorant of the love that makes the building grow....For if their knowledge had been complete, they would not have been blind to that goodness by which he willed to be born a human being, and to die for their sins.[6]

In another passage, Bernard insists that truly to know God is to fear him:

> To know him is one thing, to fear him is another; nor does knowledge make a man wise, but the fear that motivates him. Would you then call him wise who is puffed up by his own knowledge? Who but the most witless would consider those wise who, 'although they knew God, did not honor him as God or give thanks to him?'[7]

Calvin, too, as we saw above, makes this strong connection with fear of the Lord. This fear can be seen as reverential awe and not just dread, though both Bernard and Calvin sometimes also understand it in the latter sense.

In his *Institutes of the Christian Religion*, John Calvin defines faith as follows:

> Now we shall possess a right definition of faith if we call it a firm and certain knowledge of God's benevolence toward us, founded upon the truth of the freely given promise in Christ, both revealed to our minds and sealed upon our hearts through the Holy Spirit.[8]

He later goes on to say that "the knowledge of faith consists in assurance rather than in comprehension."[9] Notice how similar this is to Bernard's notion of faith as an experiential knowledge, and particularly a knowledge of God's goodness. In a later passage in the *Institutes*, Calvin says: "No one can well perceive the power of faith unless he feels it by experience in his heart."[10]

In short, one of the things that mystics—or people with a mystical sensitivity—can do for us is provide a corrective to the very cerebral way in which many Christians still approach their faith. In the first few centuries of its existence, Christianity developed in a Hellenistic (Greek) culture, which put a great stress on philosophy and often on the need to define everything precisely. It is worth repeating that there is a place for definitions of the truths of the faith. However, it has sometimes been suggested that the church made a big mistake when it shifted the critical question from "Are you in a relationship of love with Jesus?" to "Do you believe these truths that are proclaimed by the church?"

This shift has led at times to an obsession with doctrinal purity, which in its worst manifestations has resulted in things like inquisitions and heavy-handed silencings of "progressive" theologians (including a few mystics). But I suspect that Jesus finds it strange, to say nothing of unacceptable, that we Christians are sometimes willing to violate charity in order to preserve the truths of the faith. Scripture says: "Faith, hope, and love abide, these three; and the greatest of these is love" (1 Cor 13:13). It is a lesson that the church as institution still needs to learn, and the mystics can be seen as prophetic in this regard.[11]

We might summarize these reflections on love and knowledge with a statement that some of the mystics themselves were fond of: that love itself is a form of knowing.[12]

Images of God

The mystics' stress on experience is not without effect on their *conceptions* of God. This is the point to which we now turn. A particular contribution of the mystics has been with respect to *images* of God, especially feminine images. Most Christians are accustomed to thinking about and referring to God as "Father." The prayers in most mainstream Christian churches continue to use predominantly, if not exclusively, male imagery for God. It is no secret that this has driven many women out of the churches, either to form their own separate Christian communities or to reject Christianity altogether as hopelessly sexist and patriarchal.

Feminist literature on this subject abounds, and I will not attempt to give a summary of the state of this question here.[13] What concerns us is the *fact* that feminine imagery for God has a long history in the Christian tradition, and is not, contrary to the assumption of some people, a twentieth century feminist creation. The image of God as mother, for example, is not only found in scripture (see, for example, Hos 11; Is 49:14–15; 66:13; Mt 23:37; Lk 13:34–35), but also in the writings of numerous Christian authors starting from the very earliest days of the church's existence.[14] This imagery reaches a certain peak in the women mystics of the middle ages. The following pages will focus specifically on the most famous of these, Julian of Norwich.

Julian of Norwich was an English woman who lived from 1342 to about 1416. Most of what we know about her has its origin in her own book, the *Revelations of Divine Love* or "Showings." In her youth, she became preoccupied with meditating on the passion of Christ. This was not uncommon in the later middle ages. Bernard of Clairvaux and later the Franciscans stressed devotion to the humanity of Christ, and especially to his passion. The Franciscans, for example, were largely responsible for promoting the devotion of the Stations of the Cross.

At one point, Julian became ill to the point where it was feared that she would die. She was visited by a priest who counseled her to look upon the crucifix. When she did so, she received fifteen "showings" or revelations that included visions of the passion of Christ. She finally recovered, and became an anchoress—a solitary—at the Church of St. Julian in Norwich, where she lived in a cell attached to the church.

Julian became a spiritual guide for many people, who would come and speak with her through one of the two windows in her cell. (The other looked out into the church so that she could follow worship services.) She was not a scholar, and unfortunately for many centuries her work was largely disregarded (perhaps because she was a woman?). Only in our own day has there been an explosion of interest in her writings.

God as Mother

Julian's writings, like those of many other mystics, do not make for easy reading. Nevertheless, it is important to let her speak to us in her own words. The following is one of the more striking passages from *Showings*, where Julian speaks of the Trinity as Mother:

> And I saw no difference between God and our substance, but, as it were, all God; and still my understanding accepted that our substance is in God, that is to say, that God is God, and our substance is a creature in God. For the almighty truth of the Trinity is our Father, for he made us and keeps us in him. And the deep wisdom of the Trinity is

our Mother, in whom we are enclosed. And the high goodness of the Trinity is our Lord, and in him we are enclosed
and he in us. We are enclosed in the Father, and we are
enclosed in the Son, and we are enclosed in the Holy
Spirit. And the Father is enclosed in us, the Son is enclosed
in us, and the Holy Spirit is enclosed in us, almighty, all
wisdom and all goodness, one God, one Lord.[15]

This passage is remarkable for many reasons. First of all,
notice Julian's statement about God's substance and our
substance. This is something we shall return to later. Julian
says, "I saw no difference between God and our substance," but then immediately qualifies this, taking care to
assert that our substance is not in fact identical with God's.
The idea of total absorption into the divine reality has
always been looked upon with suspicion in Christianity,
especially Protestant Christianity with its strong stress on
the distance that sin creates between ourselves and God.

More interesting in the context of our present discussion
is Julian's multifaceted description of the Trinity. She associates the truth of the Trinity with the Fatherhood of God,
the wisdom of the Trinity with the Motherhood of God,
and the goodness of the Trinity with the Lordship of God.
Later, she associates these with the Father, the Son, and the
Holy Spirit respectively,[16] but it is clear to me that these categories are somewhat fluid. She speaks of them in terms of
specific persons and in terms of the Trinity as a whole.

Notice the language of enclosure that Julian uses to
describe the intimacy of our relationship with God. We are
enclosed in God, and God is enclosed in us. There is something profoundly beautiful about this notion of being
wrapped up in God and God in us. The image of a womb
comes most readily to mind here.

Julian's description of Jesus as Mother is particularly
striking:

I saw and understood that the high might of the Trinity is our Father, and the deep wisdom of the Trinity is our Mother, and the great love of the Trinity is our Lord; and all these we have in nature and in our substantial creation. And furthermore, I saw that the second person, who is our Mother, substantially the same beloved person, has now become our mother sensually, because we are double by God's creating, that is to say substantial and sensual. Our substance is the higher part, which we have in our Father, God almighty; and the second person of the Trinity is our Mother in nature in our substantial creation, in whom we are founded and rooted, and he is our Mother of mercy in taking our sensuality. And so our Mother is working on us in various ways, in whom our parts are kept undivided; for in our Mother Christ we profit and increase, and in mercy he reforms and restores us, and by the power of his Passion, his death, and his Resurrection he unites us to our substance.[17]

As I understand this passage, Julian is trying to say that Christ can be seen as our mother in terms of both our *creation* and our *redemption*. He is our mother in creation because our human nature is founded and rooted in him. This recalls that great passage from the letter to the Colossians:

He [Christ] is the image of the invisible God, the firstborn of all creation; for in him all things in heaven and on earth were created, things visible and invisible...all things have been created through him and for him. He himself is before all things, and in him all things hold together (Col 1:15–17).

At the same time, we partake of the entire Trinity in our "nature" or "substantial creation": its might, its wisdom, and its love.

Christ, however, is also "our Mother of mercy in taking our sensuality." In this respect, his role is to restore our human nature to what it was meant to be: "in mercy he reforms and restores us, and by the power of his Passion, his death, and his Resurrection he unites us to our substance." Sin, in a sense, alienates us from our true selves. Christ is our mother in *redemption* because in him we are restored.

Julian goes on to praise Mary as the source of Jesus' motherhood:

> Our Mother in nature, our Mother in grace, because he wanted altogether to become our Mother in all things, made the foundation of his work most humbly and most mildly in the maiden's womb. And he revealed that in the first revelation,[18] when he brought that meek maiden before the eye of my understanding in the simple stature which she had when she conceived; that is to say that our great God, the supreme wisdom of all things, arrayed and prepared himself in this humble place, all ready in our poor flesh, himself to do the service and the office of motherhood in everything. The mother's service is nearest, readiest, and surest: nearest because it is most natural, readiest because it is most loving, and surest because it is truest.[19]

The Politics of God-Imagery

I remember an incident that occurred when I offered the above reflections on Julian of Norwich at one of the workshops on which this book is based. It was the first time I had presented this material to a group that was not Roman Catholic. Their denomination is one that already ordains women, so I did not expect a great deal of anguish over the idea that we can speak of God as Mother.

Much to my surprise, a man in the group began to berate me for wanting to "throw out" the Father image for God and replace it with the Mother image. (I never said this; nor, as we have seen, did Julian.) He insisted that the Father image had been around for centuries (who could argue with that?) and that if Jesus could call God "Father," so should we. He was obviously quite agitated.

Indeed, this issue causes many to be agitated today. The minute anyone uses a feminine image for God, especially in a public worship service, it seems that people either get a rush of euphoria or they get angry. The question of the Motherhood of God (or any kind of feminine imagery for God) has become a political issue in the churches. In recent years, feminists and traditionalists have faced off against each other and entered into a battle that at times has been quite ugly.

There are some legitimate reasons why this issue makes so many Christians (on either side of the fence) angry or upset. But this is precisely why I find Julian of Norwich to be such a refreshing and helpful figure. Julian writes in a totally un-self-conscious way about her experiences of God. She is not trying to make a political statement. Nowhere does she suggest that the Father imagery be replaced by the Mother imagery. On the contrary, she freely and often interchangeably uses both images.

No single image can capture the mystery of God. The mystics, of all people, knew this well. Some of the mystics are famous for what we might call a fast-and-loose approach to images of God. They felt free to bounce from image to image because they knew that these were all just feeble attempts to express the inexpressible.

Nevertheless, the attempt is important. Some people today argue against any kind of personal imagery for God in order to avoid sexist language. Thus, instead of saying: "In the name of the Father, and of the Son, and of the Holy Spirit," we should begin our prayer "In the name of the Creator, Redeemer, and Sanctifier." In one famous inclusive language translation of the scriptures,[20] Christ is always referred to as the "child" of God and not the "son."

Although God is beyond personhood as we understand it, the Christian tradition has always held—and rightly so—that we can have a personal *relationship* with God. God, we hear in the first letter of John, is love (1 Jn 4:16). There is no love without relationship. Somehow, we lose something essential when we try to speak of or to God without any personal imagery. For all its problems, I think a good argument can be made that personal imagery needs to stay. In this respect, Julian, who unabashedly and unashamedly uses personal imagery, gives us good example.

This is not to suggest, however, that we just leave things as they are. Many of the Christian churches, including my own, need to be converted on this point. While I am not sure we should change the "Our Father" to "Our Father and Mother" ("Our Parent" is definitely out!), I have become convinced that we need to follow the example of mystics like Julian, who remind us that our conception of God is too small. We need to hear and use more feminine imagery for God, both in our personal and our public prayer.[21] At first it will sound strange, but after a while we will become accustomed to it. Perhaps someday we will even ask ourselves how we ever got along without it.

We can also hope that eventually this renewed use of language will contribute to changes in the structures of the churches, insofar as they continue to exclude women and perpetuate patterns of control and domination.[22] Experts in the study of language tell us that language is not only reflective of a culture, but it is also a powerful force in forming a culture. Feminists have long argued that one of the things that is holding back change in the churches is precisely the refusal to speak of God and of ourselves in new ways—as sisters and brothers, and not just "brethren," for example.

The "Negative Way"

At this point, something that was mentioned earlier bears repeating: that all our language about God is an attempt to express the inexpressible. There are actually two main traditions of mysticism that come to the fore in the late middle ages: the first is the one that we have been dealing with so far, the kind of mysticism that stresses our love for and relationship to God. It is represented by people like Bernard of Clairvaux, Julian of Norwich, Francis of Assisi, and many others. The second kind of mysticism stresses the inadequacy of *any* category, or any mixture or collection of categories, to describe God. Perhaps the most famous promoter of this kind of mysticism is Meister Eckhart. His unique approach to the knowledge of God is worth reviewing, because it complements (and does not contradict) the approach of the love-mystics.

Meister Eckhart (c. 1260–1327) was a Dominican priest who lived in the late middle ages. As a young friar, he was sent to Paris, at that time the "center of the Western intellectual world,"[23] to study theology. He later became a prominent leader in the Dominican community, as well as a popular preacher and spiritual director. Unfortunately, some of his ideas would get him into trouble with church authorities.

Eckhart often insists in his writings that we need to get beyond all "attributes" (*Eigenschaften*) if we are to achieve oneness with God. Specific characteristics are associated with multiplicity, and at bottom God is radically one. This emphasis on the stripping away of concepts explains why Eckhart's approach, and others like it, have been described in the Christian tradition as the *via negativa*, the "negative way."

Not only do *we* have to get beyond images and qualities,

however; even God must do this![24] Eckhart speaks of a "God beyond God," the radically simple One, the mystery that lurks behind all the qualities. Eckhart emphasizes that any distinctions that we make regarding God's attributes are on the side of creatures, not in God: "No difference at all is or can be found in the One, but 'all difference is below the One,' as it says in the *Fountain of Life*, Book 5."[25] In other words, we can speak of God as loving, forgiving, etc., but God as such is beyond these things.

Sometimes Eckhart even proposes the daring notion that God is not a being. He says: "If I say: 'God is a being,' it is not true; he is a being transcending being and transcending nothingness."[26] Again, "being" is an attribute that we associate with multiplicity and creaturehood. Thus, Eckhart's approach to the understanding of God can be described as a negative one, in that whatever we affirm of creatures we have to deny of God. This preserves God's uniqueness and mystery in relation to the created order.

Several scholars have pointed out that when Eckhart is properly understood in the full context of his thought, he need not be understood as a dangerous figure, but rather as one who offers valuable alternative insights into our beliefs. Eckhart in fact was accused of heresy and called by the inquisition to defend himself. Today he is recognized as one of the great spiritual masters, and the judgment that was made against him is considered to be "at least in part unsound."[27] We will be saying more about him in the chapter on union with God.

Combining the Two Approaches

Perhaps a balanced view of the question of imagery for God is one that puts the insights of Julian of Norwich and Eckhart together, and sees them as expressing a healthy tension. On the one hand, we need personal imagery for God, because we are in a relationship with the God of love. On the other hand, we need to keep in mind that God does not fit any of our images exactly, and in fact is beyond all images and all categorical descriptions.

Let us summarize the insights that we can glean from the mystics on the subject of the knowledge of God:

(1) True knowledge of God, according to the mystics, is not purely intellectual, but rather experiential. Experiencing God is in fact a form of knowing—some would say the best form. Generally, this experience of God is described in terms of love: God's love for us, and our love for God and neighbor in return.

(2) Our God is too small. We need to expand our appreciation for different images of God, especially feminine images, and at the same time recognize that no image can enclose or capture the meaning of God.

The above insights have the potential of revolutionizing our Christian lives. To think about God, and our relationship with God, in new ways is to invite the possibility of living out that relationship in new ways. This is something that both individual Christians and the churches as institutions need to do.

To accept feminine imagery for God is to raise the issue of women's roles in the churches. Since God can be both Father and Mother, since *Jesus* can be seen as Mother as well as Brother and Son, many have asked whether the exclusion of women from any ordained ministry in the church can really be justified.[28]

To accept Eckhart's insistence that God is beyond all categories is to call into question the rigid dogmatism that sometimes characterizes Christian communities. It is to be reminded that God is not contained in our categories or dogmas, and to consider the possibility that God's revelation can be made manifest wherever God wills, and for that matter not exclusively within Christianity.

What it all adds up to is this: we need to learn more humility in terms of what we claim to know about God. Christianity, while it has always in theory been a religion that values humility, has over the course of its history been guilty at times of triumphalism and a know-it-all mentality. This has been true not only of the large institutional communities like Roman Catholicism, but also of independent storefront churches. The mystics can help all of us to get off our high horses and recognize our need to stand humbly before the Mystery of mysteries.

3

Grace and Freedom

Some years ago, when I was visiting a friend who is a very devout Christian, we drove into town to pick up some things at the store. This particular town had a tremendous shortage of parking spaces, but as we rounded a corner, there was a space waiting for us. My friend exclaimed, "Oh, thank you, Jesus, for finding us this parking space!" I said nothing. As far as I was concerned, it was just plain dumb luck that we happened to come around the corner at the right time. Jesus had nothing to do with it, I thought. (Surely he has better things to do than find parking spaces for his followers!)

Recently, I recalled this incident in a homily, expressing pretty much the point of view I just mentioned. After the service, a woman took issue with me regarding Jesus and the parking space. She insisted that Jesus does indeed find parking spaces for people, and how could I say that he didn't? Maybe she is right. I hope I don't burn in hell for denying that Jesus has power over parking spaces.

Most people I know can see the humor in this incident. What they find less humorous, particularly those who are committed believers, are questions like: What *does* in fact God do for us? Are specific events "caused" by God? Are we in fact at the mercy of a certain kind of divine fate? Or, on the other hand, did God just set the universe in motion and then let it run by itself, not interacting with it in any way?

Most of the time, these are not burning questions for us. But when tragedy strikes, they often come rapidly to the fore. A ten year old child is stricken with cancer. A twenty year old college student, who is bright and energetic, is paralyzed in a car accident. A woman dies suddenly and unexpectedly, two weeks before the arrival of her first granddaughter, which she so eagerly awaited.

At these times we feel helpless, and we wonder what God is up to. We have lost control of the situation, and we anxiously seek some way of finding solace and meaning in the midst of our troubles. We might even get angry and blame God for what has happened. After all, God *must* be in control. How could God do this to us?

The person who believes that Jesus finds us parking spaces might respond with stalwart courage and insist that we have to accept whatever God sends to us, whether a parking space or a heart attack. It's all in God's hands and we have to trust that he (it's always "he" for these people) knows what he's doing. End of conversation.

But for most of us, this answer does not suffice. We have a feeling that it is a bit more complicated than that. Somehow, we cope with the tragedies when they come, and we even have a deep sense that God has been with us and has helped us through them, but after the worst tears have dried, we are still left wondering what it all means. Such is the mystery of life.

In Christian terms, the basic issue here is that of grace and freedom. What is the relationship between God's activity and our own? At the outset, let us be clear that the mystics are not going to resolve this mystery for us. Remember, they are the ones who are usually standing (or kneeling!) in awe of the mystery, not trying to figure it out.

Nevertheless, they do have some insights that can help us as we struggle to live meaningful Christian lives in the late twentieth century.

The Meaning of "Grace"

The word grace itself is in need of clarification. Christians often hear this word in church, but when you press them for a definition, they can't formulate one. In Roman Catholicism before Vatican II, grace was spoken of almost like a quantifiable substance, a kind of spiritual Gatorade that gets poured into us when we receive communion or one of the other sacraments, or when we do a good deed. This kind of an understanding of grace is surely not adequate for today, nor does it do justice to the rich theology of grace that one encounters when studying the history of Christian theology.

It is not necessary to review that history here.[1] Instead, let us recall briefly the contemporary understanding of the concept of grace that we encountered in Chapter 1. Simply stated, grace is another word for talking about the presence or self-communication of God.[2] God freely chooses to create the world and everything in it; thus her (God's!)[3] goodness and power are poured out into the created order. While God is not to be *identified* with creation (this would be pantheism), God is always present to all creation, even as God sustains the world in its very existence.

But Christians have always understood God's presence as an active presence, which brings us back to the question: What does it mean to speak of the activity of God in the world, apart from the bare fact of sustaining the world in its existence? Does God get into specific events?

The answers that the mystics propose are sure not to please everyone. In general, when they talk about God's action in the world, the medieval mystics, and medieval theologians in general, are interested in actions relating to our salvation (redemption from sin and death) and our relationship with God (usually expressed in terms of union with God). When John Calvin proceeds in the *Institutes* to discuss what God has done for us, he in fact divides his reflections into two parts: God the Creator, and God the Redeemer. He notes that God is revealed in creation, but that sin blinds us to recognizing this revelation, save for the basic recognition of God's existence and an awareness that we should be living in accordance with God's will. Notice he says *awareness*. Our conscience is able to distinguish right from wrong, but the *power* to live rightly, according to Calvin, only comes through the grace that is offered to us through Jesus Christ.[4] In all of this, Calvin is in harmony with the medieval theologians who came before him.

God's Grace and Our Response

None of this is news to those of us who have embraced Christian faith. But it still doesn't answer the question of how God's activity is related to ours. Even redemption, which Christians would all agree is the work of God, involves some kind of response on our part. The nature of that response is something that has been hotly debated for centuries.[5]

The mystics are helpful here, as they are in many other areas, in that they present us with a *balanced* perspective. Richard Kieckhefer, a distinguished scholar of the history of spirituality, offers a good summary of their approach:

> The mystics typically resist the Pelagian assurance that sheerly human effort, manifested in moral striving and

devotional activities, can lead to sanctification or salvation. Yet they just as commonly eschew the quietist extreme, which views God as the sole agent of salvation, and concludes that there is no need for human effort of any kind, whether in morals, in devotions, or in service to humanity.[6]

This balance is reflected in the bible itself, especially in the first letter of John, which exhorts us to love one another, but reminds us: "We love, because God first loved us" (1 Jn 4:19).

Bernard of Clairvaux is particularly clear on the dynamic relationship of divine and human activity. In his classic treatise *On Grace and Free Choice*, he says:

> There can be no doubt...that the beginning of our salvation rests with God, and is enacted neither through us nor with us. The consent and the work, however, though not originating from us, nevertheless are not without us.[7]

In other words, God "makes the first move" and in fact is the force behind our response; but we are not just passive automatons. We must say "yes" to God's saving action in our lives, and be willing to live out the consequences of that yes. Bernard goes on to say:

> What was begun by grace alone, is completed by grace and free choice together, in such a way that they contribute to each new achievement not singly but jointly; not by turns, but simultaneously. It is not as if grace did one half of the work and free choice the other; but each does the whole work, according to its own peculiar contribution. Grace does the whole work, and so does free choice—with this one qualification: that whereas the whole is done *in* free choice, so is the whole done *of* grace.[8]

In other words, our relationship with God is not a "50-50 proposition." God gives his all, and we must give ours.

Of course, Bernard insists that even what we give is in fact a gift from God. In his treatise *On Loving God,* he states:

> The Apostle (Paul, in 1 Cor 4:7) says to him who glorifies himself: "What have you that you have not received? And if you have received it, how can you boast of it as if you had not received it?"...We should...fear that ignorance which gives us a too low opinion of ourselves. But we should fear no less, but rather more, that which makes us think ourselves better than we are. This is what happens when we deceive ourselves [into] thinking some good is in us of ourselves....It is pride, the greatest of sins, to use gifts as if they were one's by natural right and while receiving benefits to usurp the benefactor's glory.[9]

A more poetic expression of this theme is found in the writings of another great mystic whom we have already mentioned, Francis of Assisi. In his famous "Canticle of the Creatures," Francis proclaims:

> Most high, all-powerful, good Lord,
> Yours are the praises, the glory, the honor, and all blessing.
> To You alone, Most High, do they belong,
> and no man is worthy to mention Your name.[10]

Francis goes on to praise God in all of creation, including human life (and even human death). Francis had a deep sense that all was gift.

At the same time, Francis was a man of action. He enjoined his friars and all of his sisters and brothers who joined his movement to "observe the holy gospel of our Lord Jesus Christ by living in obedience, without anything of their own, and in chastity."[11] One of the more noteworthy points that Francis makes in his Rule is that work is a *grace* or gift.[12] I find this statement remarkable for two reasons. First of all, it stands in stark contrast to the prevailing idea that work was a curse, part of the legacy of the sin of

Adam and Eve.[13] Second, it is an almost perfect illustration of Bernard's point about God's and our activity each contributing 100%. The work we do is definitely our work, yet it is at the same time entirely a grace.

Another mystic who maintained a sense of balance between God's grace and our response is Johannes Tauler, a Dominican priest who lived in the fourteenth century. Tauler, in fact, was a disciple of Meister Eckhart, to whom we have already been introduced in Chapter 2. However, he was a bit more restrained in the way he formulated his ideas, so he was never accused of heresy as his teacher was.

Tauler often stressed the idea that we are saved by God's grace and not by our own works. To give an example:

> For as long as a man is without the grace of God, he is still in his natural state, so that even if it were possible for him to perform every good deed ever done in this world, he would still be doing nothing and standing idle, and all his work would be profitless.[14]

Tauler did speak of preparing to receive the Holy Spirit, but emphasized that this preparation was itself the *work* of the Spirit:

> Let us now see what we must do to receive this gracious Holy Spirit. The most intimate and the best preparation for receiving Him must be made by the Holy Spirit Himself working in us. He Himself must prepare the place for Himself, and also He must receive Himself in us.[15]

But again, like Francis, Tauler did not intend to promote quietism. In one of his sermons he declares:

> It would be wrong to put aside everything and just wait for the Holy Ghost. If the love of God is all your joy and all your purpose, you should do everything for that love and

to His praise. Do each task in its proper order as it falls to your lot from God's hands, working with love and quiet good will, in peaceful abandonment, keeping peace in yourself and with your neighbor. It is not activity, but disordered activity, that can hinder you.[16]

And what would constitute "disordered activity"? Clearly, for Tauler, it is activity that is grounded in the wrong *attitude*, whereby we attribute to ourselves the good that we do or the progress that we make in the spiritual life:

There are some people who fall over themselves with enthusiasm as soon as they feel a pious desire to turn over a new leaf and live more virtuously. They become infatuated with their new devotion and eager to put it into practice. They never stop to wonder if they are taking on more than they can manage, or if they have been given the grace to keep it up. It is a mistake to embark on any new venture without first considering how we can carry it through. The first thing to do is always to have recourse to God. We must confide in Him and put our fervor and devotion in His hands. But no; these folk want to rush off by themselves and start all kinds of new practices; and it is this rashness which brings them to grief, because they are building on their own strength.[17]

Elsewhere, he is even clearer on this matter:

God in His wisdom has decided that He will reward no works but His own. In the kingdom of heaven it is His work that will be crowned, not yours. Anything in you that He has not wrought Himself will count for nothing.[18]

Richard Kieckhefer provides a good clarification of the dynamic relationship between God's activity and ours according to Tauler: "It appears that man himself undertakes the initial stages of spiritual ascent, but man is in fact only the secondary cause of this striving, or the instrument of God's work within the soul."[19] This idea of primary and secondary causes is one to which we will return later.

The Relevancy of the Medieval View

The medieval mystics lived in a world that was obviously very different from our own. We might be tempted to regard their reflections on God's activity and ours as quaint relics of the past. But I would suggest, to the contrary, that their contributions are as relevant now as they ever were.

In general, Christianity has affirmed the importance both of God's grace as motivating and energizing human activity, and of human decisions made in freedom. It may be that in medieval times, God's activity was stressed so much that there was a tendency to minimize the significance of human actions and decisions. The mystics, as we have seen, fought against this tendency. But perhaps today the opposite is the case. In this age of rapid advances in technology, it seems as though every day there is some new development that will make life easier or alleviate its pains. The day this paragraph was written, a story appeared about a new technique that may make a lot of heart bypass operations obsolete.[20] Over the past two centuries, scientific advances have made it easier and easier for us to get caught up in our own human accomplishments, and to think of ourselves as being able to bend nature to our own purposes.

To some extent, this deeply-engrained attitude has been implanted in western culture by Christianity. In the book of Genesis, God says to the human beings he has created: "Be fruitful and multiply, and fill the earth and subdue it; and have dominion over the fish of the sea and over the birds of the air and over every living thing that moves upon the earth" (Gen 1:28). Properly understood, this passage was not meant to give humanity a blank check to plunder and pillage the earth; rather, it made us *responsible* for the earth even as it put the earth at our disposal.

Unfortunately, Christian western culture has often treated the earth simply as a bottomless pit of resources to be exploited for our own needs. For a long time we got away with this because nature seemed to be so abundant with renewable resources. In our own day, the environment is showing dangerous signs of stress from the abuse inflicted by the human species. A new group of prophets, the environmentalists, are beginning to question whether the human race might be on the verge of extinction, the victim of its own wanton excess and carelessness. We worry now about the ozone layer and air and water pollution, and with good reason.

Perhaps now is an appropriate time, after centuries of sometimes shameless pride in our accomplishments and attempting to bend nature to our will, to recognize anew that all we have is a gift from God. Maybe the fact that we are not as much in control as we thought we were will drive us to acknowledge, with the mystics and with Psalm 24, that "the earth is the Lord's and all that is in it."

At the same time, we might reflect on the awesome *risk* that God took in creating a world whose future can at least in some degree be determined by *our* decisions. One of the great mysteries of life is that God gave us freedom of choice: a freedom that we can exercise not only in relationship to God, but also in relationship to each other and to the rest of creation. In all their attention to people's response to God's grace, the mystics were not unaware that people have the freedom to say "no" to God. This refusal to live in harmony with God's will is something that will be taken up again in the next chapter. That same freedom makes it possible for us to treat one another with cruelty and to treat the rest of the created order with callous indifference or disdain. But there is a catch.

The catch is this: while God gives us the freedom to make selfish or immoral decisions, she also lets us live with the consequences of those decisions. Several years of theological reflection have led me to the tentative conclusion that God is not going to break into history and clean up the mess that we have created.[21] It may be that God will not even step in if we are on the verge of destroying ourselves. Therein lies both the danger and the challenge of our freedom.

Moving Beyond the "God of Control"

The idea that God controls all specific events in history, which is still common among many Christians and other religious believers, is one that needs to be seriously challenged today. It is relatively innocuous to claim that "Jesus found me this parking space." It is anything but innocuous to regard the arms race, particularly the building and maintaining of nuclear arsenals, as part of God's will for the coming "tribulation," as some fundamentalists would have us believe. Indeed, I would go so far as to say that such a point of view is pernicious and even demonic.

In a deeply disturbing but significant book, *Theology for a Nuclear Age*, Gordon Kaufman asserts that the emergence of nuclear weapons must change the whole way we think about human existence if the earth as we know it is going to survive. This includes the way we think about God, Jesus, and theology. While many have expressed serious reservations about Professor Kaufman's concept of God (that we will not enter into here), he is absolutely right that we can no longer afford to approach our

Christian faith the same way it was approached before 1945. As Albert Einstein once ominously said, "Nuclear weapons have changed everything except our way of thinking." It is presumptuous of us to think that the Christian worldview is somehow exempt from re-examination, as if it were above history and impervious to modification.[22]

Where do the mystics fit into this discussion? They take it as axiomatic, based on the texts we have reviewed in this chapter, that God is not going to do for us what we must do for ourselves. To the extent that God has placed the world in our hands, we are responsible for it. In the film, "Oh God!" God (played by George Burns) is asked why he doesn't do anything about the suffering in the world. God replies, "Why don't *you* do something about it?" Later, when God is on trial, he says something like: "I gave you people everything you need to make the world work. Go to it!" So, chances are that God will not prevent a nuclear holocaust. *We* have to do that. And we should not be willing to believe for one second that a nuclear holocaust would represent in any way God's will.

A Christian Response to Evil and Suffering

Of course, there is a missing link here. Not all suffering or problems are caused by human decisions. There are natural disasters like earthquakes and tornadoes. There are diseases with which people are born, due to no apparent fault of their parents. Regrettably, the mystics do not come closer than anyone else to understanding (let alone resolving!) the problems of natural evil and innocent suffering. This is not an issue that they often address directly. Nevertheless, they do have something to say about the meaning of evil and suffering. Let us look at a few examples.

Bernard of Clairvaux, in one of his *Sermons on Psalm 90*, speaks of God's presence to us in tribulation: "O Lord, if you are with us, grant that I may always have tribulation so that I may always merit to have you with me." Bernard expresses here one of the classic Christian beliefs about suffering: that God is present to those who suffer. Jesus certainly expressed this point in the famous discourse about the last judgment, where the sheep are separated from the goats on the basis of how they responded to those in need: "Truly I tell you, just as you did it to one of the least of these who are members of my family, you did it to me" (Mt 25:40).

The cross itself can be seen as a symbol of God's solidarity with human suffering. It is noteworthy that Jesus never promised that there would be no suffering for those who follow him. On the contrary, he told his disciples to prepare for persecution and trials. While some Christians believe that God will take away any suffering if one prays with enough faith (what, one may ask, does that mean?), most of us know that some suffering does not go away, and some disasters are not avoided, even for people whose faith is profound.

Julian of Norwich, who as you recall had visions of Jesus' suffering and wanted to share in it, reflects at some length in her thirteenth revelation about human suffering, which she sees as related to sin. According to Julian, sin is known by the pain and suffering it causes. She says: "Sin is necessary but all shall be well." We will only know the "why" of sin (and perhaps also of suffering?) in heaven; for now, it is hidden in God. Julian emphasizes that we should not pry into the Lord's secrets. We need to trust that "all shall be well." God, she believes, pays attention to the great and to the small.[23]

In some ways, this answer is reminiscent of the one that God gave to Job when Job complained to him about the injustice of his being an upright follower of God's law and yet having to suffer. God begins his answer with the following words:

> Where were you when I laid the foundation of the earth?
> Tell me, if you have understanding.
> Who determined its measurements—surely you know!
> Or who stretched the line upon it?
> On what were its bases sunk,
> or who laid its cornerstone
> when the morning stars sang together
> and all the heavenly beings shouted for joy? (Job 38:4–7).[24]

God does not dispute that Job has been a good person. He does not say that Job deserves his sufferings. Finally, he calls Job to make a radical act of trust. Job does not see the "big picture"; God does. Therefore, Job is not in a position to judge God's justice based on his limited perspective.

Although this response hardly resolves the question of innocent suffering, I have come to believe that it still has relevance for us today. We, like Job, have to reckon with the ambiguity and mystery of life. Perhaps finally the difference between a religious believer and a non-believer is the confidence that, ultimately, somehow "all shall be well," and that for all of its suffering and ambiguity, life is worthwhile and has a purpose. Our belief in God grounds this confidence.[25]

God Acts Through Secondary Causes

Notice that we have not dealt yet with the question of miracles, which most people understand as God's intervention in specific situations, especially illness and disease. I can almost hear some readers saying: "Well, *what about miracles?* I know someone who was cured of [fill in the blank

with the appropriate malady] through prayer and the lay-
ing on of hands." Many Christians, of various denominations, actively seek out healing services. In my own
tradition, Roman Catholicism, there are several famous
sites of healings like Lourdes and Fatima, as well as a number of healing priests who take their healing services "on
the road."

Frankly, none of these things lead me to modify anything that has been said in this chapter. I am not saying
that I don't believe in faith-healings. I will admit that I
tend to be a skeptic about such things. I frankly have problems with the way most people talk about miracles. Either
they see them as divine interventions, interruptions of the
otherwise normal course of history, or they totally dismiss
them as superstition. The truth lies between these poles.

Recall Richard Kieckhefer's remark that, for Tauler,
God is the "primary cause" of people's growing in holiness, and people are the "secondary cause." An age-old
axiom of Roman Catholic theology says: "God always acts
through secondary causes."[26] If we accept this axiom, we
can accept a modern scientific worldview and at the same
time leave room for genuine divine activity in our midst.

To say that God always acts through secondary causes is
to acknowledge that God does not abolish or suspend the
laws of nature that she herself set up. But the limits of
those laws of nature may be much wider than most of us
suppose. We have perhaps too limited a sense of what is
naturally possible, which forces us to conclude that when
something extraordinary happens, God must have stepped
in and done the *im*possible, rather than considering that
God has worked with possibilities that exist latently, and
largely unrecognized by us, within the natural order.[27]

Interestingly, people seem to accept this idea when it
comes to psychic phenomena: that there are all kinds of

possibilities latent in the human psyche that we have not yet begun to fathom, let alone tap. We need to carry this notion over to natural phenomena too.

It is clear that sometimes, even when God gives his 100% and we give ours, the suffering and pain do not go away. Suffering and pain, like life itself, remain at bottom a mystery that we will never comprehend in this life.

Of two things we can be sure: First, God never acts in a way that impinges upon our freedom and dignity. Second, God is always present to us and aids us spiritually, even when the external situation doesn't seem to go our way. I am always more impressed with a faith healer who claims that the most important healing is spiritual. Those who stress flashy and spectacular physical healings can often, as we all know, be charlatans. Of course, physical healing does often enough take place. Why not always? The answer to this question is hidden in the mystery of God.

Conclusions

What conclusions, then, can we draw from this discussion? The mystics remind us that:

(1) God is the source of all we are and all we have, and God is actively present to all of creation. She invites human beings into a relationship of love and unity with her, with each other, and with the world. While God's grace is operative whenever we respond with a "yes," God also leaves us free to say "no" to that relationship. The mystics have their own idea as to what motivates the "no" that we often say. We will discuss this further in the next chapter.

(2) God is not going to do for us what we must do for ourselves. He took the risk of creating us as free beings, and was prepared to live with the consequences of that risk. It is interesting how we humans find this easy to

accept when things are going well, i.e., when we are "in control." But when things are out of control we want God to take over. Unfortunately, we can't have it both ways. God has made us responsible for our own decisions.[28]

(3) God is not absent from us during times of suffering and pain. On the contrary, God is especially close to us at these times. How that presence will affect the outcome of a particular crisis situation is a question that has no one answer. Some Christians seem to think that God will always give us what we pray for, as long as we pray in faith. Experience, however, does not bear this out. While physical healings and the like do take place, the fact is that suffering and pain continue in the world. Perhaps instead of blaming God for this dilemma, we should—as George Burns said in "Oh, God!"—do more to alleviate the suffering ourselves. We will see in Chapter 5 that the mystics put a great deal of stress on service to those in need.

Everything we have said in this chapter suggests that the Christian life does not just involve passive submission, but active response to God. We might find the whole thing a bit intimidating, especially if we are accustomed to thinking that we have fulfilled our responsibility to God by going to church on Sunday, being nice to our neighbor, and avoiding the seven deadly sins. But the mystics were realistic about Christian life. They knew that it took a lifetime to mature into the people that God called them to be. It is to this insight that we now turn: the notion of conversion as a lifelong process.

4

Conversion: A Lifelong Process

In his *Life of St. Francis*, Bonaventure, one of the great writers in the Franciscan tradition, tells a remarkable story. He has just finished describing Francis' retreat at Mount LaVerna. While there, Francis had a mystical vision of the cross of Christ, and was granted his wish to share in Christ's sufferings: he was given the gift of the *stigmata*, wounds in his hands, feet, and side. Bonaventure now recounts what happened when Francis came down from the mountain and rejoined his brothers and sisters in community:

> Since he could not walk because of the nails protruding from his feet, he had his half-dead body carried through the towns and villages to arouse others to *carry the cross* of Christ (Luke 9:23). He used to say to the friars: "Let us begin, brothers, to serve the Lord our God, for up to now we have hardly progressed." He was ablaze with a great desire to return to the humility he practiced at the beginning; to nurse the lepers as he did at the outset and to treat like a slave once more his body that was already in a state of collapse from his work. With Christ as his leader, he proposed to do great things; and although his limbs were failing, he bravely and fervently hoped to conquer the enemy in a new combat. Laziness and idleness have no place where the goad of love never ceases to drive a person to

greater things. His body was so much in harmony with his spirit and so ready to obey it that when he strove to attain complete holiness, his body not only did not resist, but even tried to run ahead.[1]

If we can get past the strong "passion" spirituality that this passage reflects (which we've seen before in people like Julian of Norwich) and its somewhat idealized portrait of Francis, we notice here a striking statement about him. Here was a man who had dedicated his life to living the gospel, and who had just had about as intimate an experience of union with God as was probably possible for a human being, and what was the first thing that came to his mind afterward? "Let us *begin* to serve the Lord our God, for up to now we have hardly progressed."

This stunning passage almost makes us want to say: "Surely Francis can't be serious! How can a person who has made so much progress in the spiritual life continuously talk about being a beginner?" But it was not false modesty that led Francis (and other mystics) to speak in this fashion. One of the paradoxes of the spiritual life is that the more one grows, the more sensitive one becomes to the need to grow further.

This should come as good news to those of us who are less further along in our spiritual journey. In the last chapter, we stressed that saying "yes" to God involves taking responsibility for the awesome gift of our freedom. The mystics knew that "Rome was not built in a day," however. They knew that growth in the spiritual life was a lifelong struggle, with many ups and downs. They also grasped (and this perhaps comes as the accompanying bad news) that the biggest obstacle to spiritual growth was not found outside of human beings, but within.

The Enemy Within

Most of us have probably heard the expression: "the world, the flesh, and the devil." These are the things that supposedly keep us from God. They are often conveniently trotted out when we want to excuse ourselves from wrong-doing: e.g., "the devil made me do it." But the mystics won't let us off the hook so easily. They challenge us to look into ourselves and face the real enemy: us!

In his bestselling book, *People of the Lie*, M. Scott Peck discusses at great length the connection between sin and narcissism.[2] I read this book several years after beginning my study of mysticism. The thought struck me that Dr. Peck was not exactly expounding a new revelation here. The medieval mystics made much the same point centuries ago.

The basic obstacle to growth in grace, according to the mystics, is self-will. Francis of Assisi was acutely aware of this. In the second of his "Admonitions," a document that presents a summary of his spirituality, Francis says to his community:

> The Lord said to Adam: Eat of every tree; do not eat of the tree of the knowledge of good and evil (cf. Gen 2:16–17). He was able to eat of every tree of paradise since he did not sin as long as he did not go against obedience. For the person eats of the tree of the knowledge of good who appropriates to himself his own will and thus exalts himself over the good things which the Lord says and does in him; and thus, through the suggestion of the devil and the transgression of the command, what he eats becomes for him the fruit of the knowledge of evil. Therefore it is necessary that he bear the punishment.[3]

In fact, we have already spoken about self-will in Chapter 3: is this not what is behind our treating the world as if it finally belongs to us and is not "on loan" to us from God?

Another text that gets to the heart of this matter is the *Theologia Germanica,* an anonymous work of the fourteenth century that seems to have emerged from a circle with which John Tauler was connected. (He is, in fact, quoted in the work.)[4] The *Theologia Germanica* states flatly that the essence of sin is self-will:

> We are used to saying that Adam was lost and fell because he ate the apple.
>
> I say it was because of his presumption and because of his I and his Mine, his Me and the like.[5]

The perversity of self-will is such that we can be deceived into thinking that we can persist in it and still find the way to God:

> We wish to be stroked, as it were; there is in us a strong longing for pleasure and sweetness and enjoyment and in the very experience of it we believe that all is well and that we love God.[6]

But in fact, this self-love is disobedience,[7] and it must be cleared away if the life of God is going to take root in us.

Stages in the Spiritual Life

The process of growing in the spiritual life has often been described in terms of distinct stages or steps. A particularly insightful portrayal of these stages (though it is only one of many in the history of Christian mysticism) is offered by Bernard of Clairvaux, in his treatise *On Loving God.* It is worth reviewing in some detail.

Bernard speaks of four stages by which we come to love God. The first stage is loving ourselves for our own benefit. The second is loving God for our own benefit. The third is loving God for God's sake. The final stage is where we love even ourselves for God's sake.

Before he gets into discussing these stages, however, Bernard asks the question: Why should we love God? His answer echoes a theme that we have already encountered:

> Hence when seeking why God should be loved, if one asks what right he has to be loved, the answer is that the main reason for loving him is "He loved us first."[8]

Bernard goes on to make the statements about the primacy of God's grace that we discussed in Chapter 3.[9] He further states that "we must love God without any limit," because God has "loved us so much and so freely, insignificant as we are and such as we are." At this point, he inserts a prayer:

> My God, my help, I shall love you as much as I am able for your gift. My love is less than your due, yet not less than I am able, for even if I cannot love you as much as I should, still I cannot love you more than I can. I shall only be able to love you more when you give me more, although you can never find my love worthy of you.[10]

Notice how this prayer expresses Bernard's awareness that we will never reach a point (at least not in this life) where we can say that we love God enough.

Let us look then at each of the four stages that Bernard has laid out in his treatise:

(1) Loving ourselves for our own benefit: Bernard begins by saying that since nature is "fragile and weak,"[11] we necessarily love ourselves first, and for our own sake. Incidentally, Bernard does not want to say that this love is bad. On the contrary, it is good, as long as it remembers the commandment, "Love your neighbor as yourself" (Mt 22:39). Whatever rights we claim for ourselves, we must

remember that our neighbors have the same rights. Bernard distinguishes in this section of his treatise between "just needs" and "pleasures," and he cautions against pitting one's own pleasures against the just needs of others:

> Your love will be sober and just if you do not refuse your brother that which he needs of what you have denied yourself in pleasure. Thus carnal love becomes social when it is extended to others.[12]

In trying to attend to our neighbors' needs, however, we find that we come up short. We realize that we do not have what is necessary to love with "perfect justice." Thus we are moved to begin loving God, knowing that without God we can do nothing good.[13]

A few comments are in order here. It is uncanny how Bernard writes almost as if he were aware of our twentieth century problem with distinguishing needs and wants. The advertising media have duped us into believing that we "must" have certain things in order to be happy. When we look honestly at these claims, however, we realize that we don't really need most of these things. It is always sobering to remind ourselves that the human race survived for centuries without many of the things that we regard as necessities today.

Bernard's most striking insight here is that it is possible for some people's genuine needs to remain unfulfilled precisely because other people are gorging themselves on wants. I once heard a young person say: "There is no such thing as having too much." We'd like to believe that, wouldn't we? But how do we deal with the *fact* that in our complex world today, there is no such thing as some people having too much without other people having too little? The Christian can give no other response than to insist

that every human being is entitled to have certain fundamental needs fulfilled.[14]

But how hard it is to break out of the addiction to having more and more things! Particularly in American culture, the pattern of material accumulation is so deeply
engrained in us that we believe we have a right to everything we can get. It indeed takes more than personal will
power to begin to overcome the self-centeredness that our
culture reinforces in us every day. Even with the power of
God's love and grace behind us, it's hard to "let go."

Thus, several centuries later, we who are trying to "love
our neighbor as ourselves" can see the logic of Bernard's
shift to the second stage. We come to realize that we need
God's help to love rightly, and so we move to:

(2) Loving God for our own benefit: Bernard does not
dwell very long on this stage. He notes that initially we
turn to God for what he can do for us. But eventually that
selfish motivation changes:

> If man's tribulations, however, grow in frequency and as a
> result he frequently turns to God and is frequently freed by
> God, must he not end, even though he had a heart of stone
> in a breast of iron, by realizing that it is God's grace which
> frees him and come to love God not for his own advantage
> but for the sake of God?[15]

Thus we are moved to the third stage, where we love God
for God's sake.

An analogy might be drawn here to the way a human
relationship of love grows. We know that initially, in both
friendship and courtship, we tend to be attracted to a relationship for selfish reasons. We start a relationship
because, for whatever reason, it gives us pleasure to be
around this particular person. If the relationship is to grow
into a real friendship or a commitment such as marriage,

however, we know that it has to move beyond what that person can do for us to a genuine appreciation, love, respect, and acceptance of the other *as other.*

A few centuries before Christianity, the Greek philosopher Aristotle, in his *Nichomachean Ethics*, spoke of different kinds of friendship. The first two kinds are both fundamentally motivated by self-centeredness: we love others for their utility, i.e., for the good that they can bring to us, or for the pleasure that they can bring to us. Utility and pleasure are fleeting things, and thus these friendships often do not last. Perfect friendship, however, is reached by those who "wish well to their friends for their [i.e., the friends'] sake."[16] It is based on an acceptance of the other that transcends jealousy and competition, which delights in the other's uniqueness and goodness. Bernard's description of the shift to the third stage is not all that different.

(3) Loving God for God's sake: Bernard first describes how it is God's own sweetness that lures us into this stage:

> Man's frequent needs oblige him to invoke God more often and approach him more frequently. This intimacy moves man to taste and discover how sweet the Lord is. Tasting God's sweetness entices us more to pure love than does the urgency of our own needs.[17]

Again, is this not the miracle of true love, when someone else's goodness draws us out of our self-centeredness and moves us to centeredness in another or in others? It is at this stage, Bernard claims, that people will not have trouble *properly* fulfilling the command to love their neighbors:

> A man who feels this way will not have trouble in fulfilling the commandment to love his neighbor. He loves God truthfully and so loves what is God's. He loves purely and he does not find it hard to obey a pure commandment, purifying his heart, as it is written, in the obedience of

love. He loves with justice and freely embraces the just commandment. This love is pleasing because it is free. It is chaste because it does not consist of spoken words but of deed and truth. It is just because it renders what is received. Whoever loves this way, loves the way he is loved, seeking in turn not what is his but what belongs to Christ, the same way Christ sought not what was his, but what was ours, or rather, ourselves.[18]

This is the kind of love that is truly selfless. It is the kind of love Jesus was talking about when he said: "Love one another as I have loved you" (Jn 15:12).

Martin Luther once commented on this type of love (without making reference to Bernard, though he does mention him at other times). In his famous reformation treatise, "The Freedom of a Christian," Luther first hammers away at the idea that only the grace of God received through faith, and not good works, can bring us salvation. Having said this, he goes on to talk about the importance of good works in our relations with one another. Luther comments that since works are not needed for salvation, the whole life of persons of faith becomes an overplus—all our energies can be directed into service of others, without regard to "what's in it for us."[19] Even if one has difficulties with Luther's overall understanding of the relationship between faith and works, this is a marvelous insight.

Bernard was of the opinion that this third stage of loving God was the highest that human beings could attain during this life:

> No doubt man remains a long time in this degree, and I doubt if he ever attains the fourth degree during this life, that is, if he ever loves only for God's sake. Let those who have had the experience make a statement; to me, I confess, it seems impossible.[20]

In other places, he does speak of exceptions to this. For example, he suggests that martyrs might receive a taste of the fourth stage of love while still in their bodies.[21] In his *Sermons on the Song of Songs*, he refers several times to experiences of rapture or ecstasy, even claiming to have had them himself.[22] But he insists that these are rare and fleeting phenomena, and that *staying* in the fourth stage of love is something that happens only in the after-life.

Imagine, though, if we could achieve even this third stage of love in our lives today. In our best moments, we probably do achieve it. But we know that it is hard to sustain this kind of selfless love in our culture. Perhaps for us, it is *this* level that we seem to attain only in rare and fleeting moments! Here is where we need to remind ourselves of Francis of Assisi's exhortation: "Let us begin again!" But Bernard was not naive either; he knew well that even reaching the third stage of love was a lifelong process.

The *Theologia Germanica* offers an insight that is relevant to Bernard's discussion here. Its author remarks that sin, which is the root of our spiritual problems, is never totally rooted out in this life. Nevertheless, considerable progress can be made:

> I grant you, then, that no one lives totally and purely in...obedience, the way Christ did. It is, however, possible for man to approach and come so close to it that he can be called—and can in fact be—godly and divinized.
>
> And the closer man approaches divine obedience and the more godly and divinized he becomes, the more he will feel the pain over disobedience, sin, and unrighteousness, and the more such waywardness will hurt him and the more keenly he will suffer.[23]

Notice again the paradox that we mentioned at the beginning of this chapter: the more one progresses in the spiritual life, the more one is sensitive to the ways in which she or he still needs to grow. The *Theologia Germanica* speaks of the "spiritually illumined" as people who have an insatiable desire to grow further in their life with God:

> Mark this: Illumined people, living in the true light, perceive that everything they might desire or elect is nothing compared to that which has always been desired or elected by all creatures in the depth of their being.
>
> This realization leads them to let go of all desire and reliance on worldly things, surrendering themselves and all to the eternal Good.
>
> Yet there remains in them a desire to advance toward and to get closer to the eternal Good, by a deeper knowledge, a more burning love, a greater preparedness and more complete surrender, and a fuller obedience—and this in such a manner that each illumined person would say: "Would that I were united with the eternal Good as the hand is part of the body."[24]

Clearly, the medieval mystics equate the goal of the spiritual life with union with God. There is much more to say about this topic, which will occupy our attention in Chapter 6. For now, let us continue with Bernard's last stage.

(4) Loving even ourselves for God's sake: Bernard speaks glowingly of this crowning stage of love:

> Since Scripture says that God made everything for his own purpose, the day must come when the work will conform to and agree with its Maker. It is therefore necessary for our souls to reach a similar state in which, just as God willed everything to exist for himself, so we wish that neither ourselves nor other beings to have been nor to be except for his will alone; not for our pleasure. The satisfaction of our wants, chance happiness, delights us less than to see his will done in us and for us, which we implore every day in prayer saying: "...your will be done on earth as

it is in heaven...." O pure and sacred love! O sweet and pleasant affection! O pure and sinless intention of the will, all the more sinless and pure since it frees us from the taint of selfish vanity, all the more sweet and pleasant, for all that is found in it is divine. It is deifying to go through such an experience.[25]

It is at this stage that the believer becomes *unus spiritus*, one spirit with God.[26] Bernard in fact goes on at this point to describe more precisely the nature of this union, as we shall see later. One thing that should be noted is that for Bernard, the fourth stage of love must await not only the after-life, but the final resurrection. Medieval theologians sometimes spoke of a separation of body and soul at the time of death, with an expectation that the two would be reunited again at the last judgment. Thus Bernard says that in the interim, the soul is, as it were, distracted from full communion with God by its desire to reunite with the flesh.[27]

Life with God: A Dynamic Relationship

Contemporary theology tends to speak more of a continuing dynamic relationship of each person with God after death, rather than a separation and later a reunion of body and soul. In fact, theologians like Karl Rahner suggest that we will never really arrive at a state of perfect assimilation of the love of God, or of absolute union with God. God will always be a mystery to us, and will always be before us inviting us to "come closer," even in eternity.[28] This is an idea that, to my knowledge, is not developed by the medieval mystics.

All of this, of course, is speculation. No mystic, theologian, or believer can know the specifics of what our life with God is going to be like after death. I myself find the notion of a process of growth that continues into eternity intriguing, and not inconsistent with the overall teaching of the mystics. In any case, one important insight that we can glean from Bernard's description of the fourth stage of love is that we should neither forget about nor put too much emphasis on the after-life in our life with God.

There is, on the one hand, a danger of putting *too* much emphasis on the here and now. We can put so much stress on living for today that we ignore the fact that our present life on this earth does not go on forever (until the death of a loved one shocks us back into reality). We would do well to heed the advice of a sign I saw recently: "Live each day as if it were your last; someday you'll be right!" Some of us have probably entertained the question of what we would do if we suddenly found out we had only twenty-four hours, or six months, to live. I suspect that we would live those days with a different attitude, even if we insist that we wouldn't change any of our plans.

On the other hand, some Christians have interpreted the gospel as promising spiritual fulfillment *only* in the after-life, after we have struggled through—in the words of an old Catholic prayer—this "vale of tears," i.e., life on earth. This conviction can lead to a rather joyless Christianity that we can seriously doubt Jesus ever intended for his followers. In contrast, consider the case of Francis of Assisi, who could rejoice in all the gifts of God's creation that we can enjoy in this life—sun, moon, fire, water, earth, and all living things—and at the same time praise God for "Sister Death, from whose embrace no mortal can escape."[29]

In short, the mystics, while they always kept eternal life in mind, were people who generally lived in the present. The most important thing to them, as it should be now to us, was to grow in their relationship with God each and every day. Bernard clearly saw the third stage of love as the one that we should be aiming for in this life. If we do this, the fourth stage will take care of itself.

A comment by Julian of Norwich summarizes well the balance we find in the mystics between the present and future orientations of the Christian life. In one of her chapters of *Showings*, she writes:

> For even though our Lord God dwells now in us, and is here with us, and embraces us and encloses us for his tender love, so that he can never leave us, and is nearer to us than tongue can tell or heart can think, still we can never cease from mourning and weeping, seeking and longing, until we see him clearly, face to his blessed face, for in that precious sight no woe can remain, no well-being can be lacking.[30]

Clearly, Julian does not devalue our present existence in terms of its potential for intimacy with God. At the same time she points with longing to the future, when we will see God face to face.

Earlier we saw that Bernard's schema is only one of several approaches to understanding the stages of the spiritual life.[31] In practice, our life with God seldom evolves in an ordered sequence such as Bernard describes in *On Loving God*. Assuredly, we do not always move forward in our relationship with God. Bernard, of course, was aware of this. He knew that sin and backsliding were always possibilities. In fact, one of his most famous lines was: "Either you must go up or you must come down; you inevitably fall if you try to stand still."[32] For him, there was no such thing as "holding steady" in the spiritual life. One was either going forward or backward.

In general, it can be said that the medieval mystics had no illusions about a "pie-in-the-sky" spirituality. They were realistic about the Christian life; they knew it involved struggle and sacrifice. How can this insight help us today?

When we get discouraged in our life of faith, we might remember that struggle is part of the bargain. Jesus, after all, never promised us that following him would be easy. On the contrary, he proclaimed: "If any want to become my followers, let them deny themselves and take up their cross and follow me. For those who want to save their life will lose it, and those who lose their life for my sake, and for the sake of the gospel, will save it" (Mk 8:35).

M. Scott Peck begins his best-selling book, *The Road Less Traveled*, with a three-word paragraph: "Life is difficult."[33] He goes on to say that many people make their problems worse because they refuse to accept this proposition. It is certainly true that in our society, the advertising media continuously work on fostering the illusion that life *should* be easy. In fact, they offer us all kinds of things that promise to make life easier and more enjoyable. Sometimes the things they try to sell us under this pretext are in fact dangerous to our health and well-being.[34]

When we are honest with ourselves, we know that for all its joys, life is simply *not* going to be easy. I would go so far as to say that if we never experience the Christian life as a struggle, maybe there is something missing in our spirituality. Maybe we are avoiding some of the hard challenges of the gospel, or refusing to deal with some important questions, even doubts, in our life of faith. Frankly, I am always suspicious of people who say that they have never struggled with their faith. They say they have accepted Jesus, and since then, everything has been wonderful. One wonders how deep and how strong their faith really is. As the book of Sirach once put it:

My child, when you come to serve the Lord,
prepare yourself for testing.
Set your heart right and be steadfast,
and do not be impetuous in time of calamity.
Cling to [God] and do not depart,
so that your last days may be prosperous.
Accept whatever befalls you,
and in times of humiliation be patient.
For gold is tested in the fire,
and those found acceptable, in the furnace of humiliation.
Trust in him, and he will help you;
make your ways straight, and hope in him (Sir 2:1-6).

This passage proclaims both the hard reality of struggle, and the firm hope that God is always beside us to move us forward—even when we may think we are moving nowhere or backward!

Many Christians reach a point in their spiritual life where they feel they have hit a roadblock. All of their progress up to that point seems to be for nought. They can't get excited anymore about their prayer life or even about their service to others. It almost seems as if God has abandoned them. This stage in the spiritual journey was named "the dark night of the soul" by John of the Cross, a sixteenth century Spanish Carmelite mystic. John saw this dark night as a period of *passive* purification, in which God takes the initiative to move a person to a new level of spiritual maturity.[35]

In the midst of a spiritual crisis, it is sometimes hard to remember that God is by our side and indeed that God is doing his part to move us forward even as we are doing ours. Remember, God will not do our part for us! But at the point where our resources run dry and we are in the worst throes of the "dark night," God's grace will lift us up, if only we are open to it. I believe this because I have experienced it myself.

Application: Lifetime Commitments

I would like to close this chapter by discussing one of the most significant aspects of the Christian life as process: making a life-commitment. The night before I was going to take my solemn vows as a Franciscan—when I would commit myself for the rest of my life—one of the brothers, Ken Walsh,[36] said to me: "Dennis, don't get too excited about the vows you're going to take tomorrow. The day you *really* take solemn vows is the first day you seriously think about leaving the order somewhere down the line, and you decide to stay."

Those words have rung in my ears many times since then. They can apply not only to the vowed life in a religious community, but to any major life commitment. I *have* occasionally met friars who say that they never once thought of leaving the order, and that they have absolutely no regrets about their decision to join. I have even met some married couples who say that they have never once thought of separating. Alas, I suspect that most of us cannot count ourselves among these hearty souls. Most of us have had to struggle at times to remain faithful to our commitments. We can at least take consolation in the fact that we are not alone in this struggle.

People who have taken vows in religious communities, if they are open and caring in their relationships with others, usually sooner or later find themselves falling in love with someone—yes, even after solemn vows or ordination. When this happens, they often find that their deeply-ingrained desires for female or male companionship and for children of their own come again to the surface, and they begin to question whether they made the right decision in choosing the celibate life. Similarly, people who are married sometimes have to deal with being attracted to a person other than their spouse, or with the desire to enjoy once again the freedom that they had as single persons. These situations have the potential of disrupting our lives to the core, and it takes a great deal of divine grace and human will power to maintain our commitment instead of "seeking new pastures."

Perhaps an equally big threat to our remaining faithful, however, comes from another direction: our reaction to wrongs that are done to us. Some years ago, a friend of mine had a terrible experience of betrayal by some members of his religious community. In his anger, pain, and disillusionment, he came very close to packing his bags and leaving his order. Ironically, he received a job offer at just this time, which seemed almost to be a sign from heaven that this was the right decision. His friends kept asking him: "Is this really what you want?" After much soul-searching, he came to the realization that he truly meant what he said when he took solemn vows. He decided that he had to stay and work things out: not just for himself, but for the sake of the community and the people he had encountered in his ministry.

He later recounted that as he struggled to regain his own sense of trust, he found himself better able to empathize with others who had experienced a crisis of betrayal. Somehow, God's grace *had* touched this painful situation and brought some good out of it. Although in the midst of the crisis he felt as though God was absent, God was in fact working overtime in strange and mysterious ways to see him through the "dark night." Only when the dust cleared was he able to see how the hand of God had guided him through the crisis.

Anyone who has ever made a long-term commitment to a particular way of life probably has a story or two to tell like the ones just described. The fact is, when we make a significant commitment, we do so not only once, but over and over again. There are times when, for the greater good of all concerned, we must break certain commitments (even marriages or solemn vows), because they prove to be unsalvageable, for whatever reason. But I wonder if, as members of a society that wants instant gratification, we are often too quick to run away when the going gets tough. We don't want our life as Christians to be a process; we want everything to be as it should be right *now*—otherwise, we start looking for the door. When this happens, we put up roadblocks to God's grace. God often can find a way to write straight with our crooked lines—but we have to give God the chance!

It is also important to remember that we do not make our commitments in isolation from others. This complicates things, for our sisters and brothers in faith also have *their* ups and downs in the spiritual life. They, too, make mistakes; they, too, lose perspective. We know how easy it is to hurt each other. On the other hand, we can do a great deal to help each other on our respective spiritual journeys. One of the things that my friend came to realize during his crisis of betrayal was that the whole community was not to blame for the actions of a few. He needed to be reminded of the many people who were "for" him and who could be trusted.

I myself have found that the majority of people among whom I have lived have helped, not hindered, my spiritual life. Precisely in sharing our struggles, and in being there for one another at difficult times, we can help each other to grow.

In this connection, it is important to remember that the

task of conversion of which this chapter speaks applies not only to individual Christians but to the church as a community, and indeed as an institution. As we know, institutional conversion is slow and ponderous. Institutions with a long history, like my own Roman Catholic community, often give the impression of being dragged, kicking and screaming, into the future. It is of course also true that at their best, the institutional churches have provided a supportive and nurturing environment for the Christian life.

Sometimes it would help all of us to be more patient both with ourselves and with each other. Life is, indeed, difficult. The spiritual journey is hard. But those who join together and embrace the challenge will not regret it. The result will be a deep communion with God, with others, and with the whole of creation. What better way do we have to describe heaven?

"Sisters and brothers, let us begin to serve the Lord our God, for up to now we have hardly progressed."

5

Contemplation and Action

You may recall the cynic's definition of mysticism that was mentioned in Chapter 1: that it "begins in mist, centers in an 'I,' and ends in schism." According to this understanding, mystics are reduced to self-centered, anti-institutional "space cadets." I hope that the previous chapters have dispelled much of this misconception. I have tried to show that the classic mystics of the middle ages have much to offer to the wider Christian community, and that they are not just an elite group whose message is relevant only to themselves or to each other.

It is true that many mystics get caught up in the desire to have as intense a personal experience of God as possible. They sometimes talk at great length about the process that leads to an experience of ecstasy or union with God. The language they use to describe this process can at times sound not only personal, but individualistic, as if they no longer need the community of faith as a context for their relationship with God.

But it would be wrong to conclude from this that the mystics—for all their helpful insights into images of God, grace and freedom, and the Christian life as process—are people who, finally, are closed in on themselves, who do not really walk the same path to God as the rest of the Christian community. There have been a few mystics to whom this criticism may indeed apply; they do not include any who have been mentioned in this book. On the contrary, we shall see that most of the classic mystics, even if they sometimes had their heads in the clouds, also kept their feet on the ground: the same ground that everyone else walked.

In this chapter, we will discuss the mystics' views of the relationship between contemplation and action. Particularly with regard to this topic, it is very important to get a grasp of the entire context of a mystic's writings, lest one focus on certain texts to the exclusion of others, and end up with a skewed understanding of her or his thought. Unfortunately, much criticism of the mystics falls short in precisely this respect.

The Meaning of "Contemplation"

First we need to clarify the term "contemplation." Like mysticism, contemplation can be a slippery term. Evelyn Underhill captures its essence in speaking of it as "those developed states of introversion in which the mystic attains somewhat: the results and rewards of the discipline of Recollection and Quiet." Contemplation involves the "turning of our attention from that crisp and definite world of multiplicity" to "an experience of the All, and this experience seems...to be *given* rather than attained."[1]

Thus, contemplation has to do with a total centering of one's attention on God. It often involves the practice of certain spiritual disciplines, as Underhill mentions. Perhaps most important of all is her point that the experience seems to be *given* rather than attained. The mystics have sometimes been accused of trying to lay claim to an experience of union with God, or even to try to bring it about by their own efforts at spiritual discipline. But as we already saw in Chapter 3, the medieval mystics are very careful to stress that grace is the source of all spiritual progress, and indeed is the very ground of our response to God in faith, hope, and love.

Certainly, the medieval mystics see contemplation—especially when it brings one to an intense experience of union with God—as a highly desirable aspect of the spiritual life. Some of them even go so far as to say that contemplation is *the* most desirable goal of the spiritual life. Bernard of Clairvaux is particularly noted for this kind of emphasis.

Bernard and Contemplation

Bernard believes that the contemplative life is to be preferred to the active, because it focuses completely on love of God, which in his view is the highest form of love, surpassing even love of neighbor. In expounding his view of this subject, Bernard reveals a bias that conflicts directly with this book's thesis that there is a sense in which mysticism—in both its active and contemplative dimensions—is for everyone. Bernard, while not outright denying that this is possible, unquestionably thinks that the monastery or convent is that place where contemplative experience is most likely to happen, because there "one lives undisturbed by the cares of the world and the anxieties of life."[2]

At times Bernard is so forceful in his arguments for the monastic life that one commentator remarks: "We would be tempted to say, if we did not know better, that for St. Bernard there could be no salvation except within monastery walls."[3] Bernard makes no bones about his belief that contemplation cannot be enjoyed by all Christians. As he puts it in one of his sermons, "For it is not within the power of everybody in the Church to examine the mysteries of the divine will or of themselves to pierce the depths of God." On the other hand, Bernard goes on to say that such an experience is not necessary either, for one always has recourse to Jesus: "If...this [i.e., contemplation] is not possible to someone, let him place before him Jesus and him crucified."[4] Bernard is emphatic that faith is what is most important in our relationship with God. He even says in one place that those whose faith is strong have no need for a contemplative experience.[5] Bernard's strong, at times even one-sided, apologetic for the monastic life is somewhat tempered by these texts.

If we can look beyond the elitism of Bernard's monastic bias, we can gain much from his insights about the relationship between contemplation and action. A key text here is his fiftieth sermon on the Song of Songs. Bernard begins by asserting that "Love exists in action and in feeling." By "feeling" he means the affective love of contemplation. Bernard does not hesitate to say that this love is to be more highly valued than active love:

> Now the active prefers what is lowly, the affective what is lofty. For example, there is no doubt that in a mind that loves rightly, the love of God is valued more than love of men, and among men themselves the more perfect [is esteemed] more than the weaker, heaven more than earth, eternity more than the flesh.

This is a pretty direct statement about the love of God taking precedence over all other loves. However, Bernard immediately goes on to qualify this statement, telling the reader that in *practice*, active love usually—and rightly—takes precedence:

> In well-regulated action, on the other hand, the opposite order frequently or even always prevails. For we are more strongly impelled toward and more often occupied with the welfare of our neighbor; we attend our weaker brothers

with more exacting care; by human right and very necessity
we concentrate more on peace on earth than on the glory
of heaven; by worrying about temporal cares we are not
permitted to think of eternal things; in attending almost
continually to the ills of our body we lay aside the care of
our soul; and finally, in accord with the saying of the
Apostle, we invest our weaker members with greater honor,
so fulfilling in a sense the word of the Lord: 'the last shall
be first and the first last.' Who will doubt that in prayer a
man is speaking with God? But how often, at the call of
charity, we are drawn away, torn away, for the sake of those
who need to speak to us or be helped! How often does
dutiful repose yield dutifully to the uproar of business!...A
preposterous order; but necessity knows no law.

Bernard believes that this kind of love in action is "swayed
not by worldly values but by human needs." Thus, it is not
a betrayal of one's love for God, but is rather an expression of that love, for, as Bernard puts it, "true love is found
in this, that those whose need is greater receive first."[6]

None of this stops Bernard from saying that active love
is a step to affective love. At least *in theory*, he wants to
hold on to the priority of the latter. However, it would not
be fair to say that Bernard wishes to devalue active love.
On the contrary, he insists that active people are also better contemplatives:

After a good work one rests more securely in contemplation, and the more a man is conscious that he has not
failed in works of charity through love of his own ease, the
more faithfully will he contemplate things sublime and
make bold to study them.[7]

Bernard insists that when all is said and done, what really
matters is that God's will is done at all times.[8] More often
than not, this will mean putting aside our own desire to

rest quietly in God's presence in order to work in the "noisy" environment where God's needy people are found.

The question of a balance between the contemplative and active life was addressed by many other mystics in the period with which this book deals. For the remainder of this chapter, we will focus on two: Meister Eckhart and Teresa of Avila.

Eckhart: Detachment Without Contemplation

Meister Eckhart's contribution to this subject is best appreciated through a look at one of his most famous German sermons, which deals with the story of Jesus' visit to the home of Martha and Mary (Lk 10:38–42). Let us first review the scriptural text:

> Now as they went on their way, Jesus entered a certain village, where a woman named Martha welcomed him into her home. She had a sister named Mary, who sat at the Lord's feet and listened to what he was saying. But Martha was distracted by her many tasks; so she came to him and asked, "Lord, do you not care that my sister has left me to do all the work by myself? Tell her then to help me." But the Lord answered her, "Martha, Martha, you are worried and distracted by many things; there is need of only one thing. Mary has chosen the better part, which will not be taken away from her."

Eckhart's interpretation of this passage can only be described as fanciful. He turns the meaning of the story completely on its head, and makes Martha, not Mary, the one to be emulated. Eckhart interprets Martha's plea to Jesus (to tell Mary to help her) as follows:

> She [Martha] realized that Mary had been overwhelmed by a desire for the complete fulfillment of the soul. Martha

knew Mary better than Mary Martha, for Martha had lived
long and well, and living gives the most valuable kind of
knowledge.[9]

In Eckhart's view, Mary is "stuck" in the contemplative
state, since she is preoccupied with the fulfillment of her
soul, while Martha has moved beyond this to what really
counts: the business of virtuous living, which he will
describe more fully later in the sermon.

Eckhart continues to reflect on Mary's desire for the
enjoyment of spiritual pleasures:

Mary was so full of longing. She longed for she knew not
what, and wanted she knew not what. We harbor the suspicion that dear Mary was sitting there more for enjoyment
than for spiritual profit. Therefore Martha said, "Lord, tell
her to get up," because she feared that she would remain
stuck in this pleasant feeling and would progress no
further.[10]

According to Eckhart, "Martha stood in lordly, well-
founded virtue with a free spirit unimpeded by anything."
What then does Christ mean when he tells her that only
one thing is necessary? "What is the one thing necessary?
It is the One that is God. That is necessary for all creatures. If God were to withdraw all that is his, all creatures
would turn into nothing." Mary, "clinging to consolation
and sweetness," had not yet attained this realization.
Eckhart then paraphrases Christ's statement that Mary has
chosen the better part: this is "as if to say, 'Cheer up,
Martha; this will leave her. The most sublime thing that
can happen to a creature shall happen to her: She shall
become as happy as you.'"[11]

What Martha had achieved, according to Eckhart, is that
she "was so grounded in being that her activity did not
hinder her. Work and activity led her to eternal happi-

ness."[12] Martha, then, had so detached herself from spiritual pleasures that she was able to serve God through practicing true virtue. Eckhart is clear that this is the goal of the Christian life:

> Now some people want to go so far as to achieve freedom from works. I say this cannot be done. It was not until the time when the disciples received the Holy Spirit that they began to perform virtuous deeds. "Mary sat at the feet of the Lord and listened to his words," and learned, for she had just been put into school and was learning to live. But afterwards, when she had learned and Christ had ascended into heaven and she received the Holy Spirit, then she really for the first time began to serve. Then she crossed the sea, preached, taught, and became the servant and washerwoman of the disciples.[13]

Notice that Eckhart says that Martha is "grounded in being." This reflects his tendency toward more of a mysticism of identity than of relationship, which we will discuss more fully in the next chapter. But being grounded in God does not remove us from the world; rather, it makes it possible for us to live in the world as true disciples.

So, contrary to what we might expect from Eckhart—the one who tells us we must become totally detached in order to achieve union with God—he does not think of the contemplative dimension of the spiritual life as superior. In fact, it seems clear that he doesn't even regard it as necessary, not even as a step to the active life! Eckhart clearly sees union with God as rooted in an *attitude* of detachment; this union in turn grounds an active life of service to others. Mystical union, then, is something that is lived out in the context of our ordinary daily activities, not a separate kind of experience.[14]

Eckhart's apparent rejection of the contemplative life need not disturb us. We might more profitably look upon it as a corrective to the tendency to turn in upon ourselves in the spiritual life. The Christian life, finally, is other-directed, and Eckhart's mysticism is a stark reminder of this. We are not Christians because we want to enjoy spiritual fireworks, but so that we might empty ourselves for others as Jesus did.

This observation may have special relevance to Roman Catholics who were raised during the age of "devotional Catholicism." It is tempting to focus our spirituality on devotional practices that are very meaningful and fulfilling to us personally (praying the rosary, attending daily mass, etc.). But there is always a danger that the spiritual nourishment we draw from these things will become an end in itself. Some Catholics thus came to believe that multiplying devotions was a guarantee of spiritual growth. The truth of the matter is that growth takes place when our contemplative and active lives are integrated: when our prayer life feeds our life of service to one another, and vice versa, as we saw in an earlier quotation from Bernard.

Teresa: Another "Active Contemplative"

Teresa of Avila (1515–1582) is another mystic who has important insights to offer on the question of contemplation and action. Teresa is one of the most beloved and well-known mystics in the history of Christianity. For the "marvelous profundity" of her teaching, she was declared a doctor of the church by Pope Paul VI in 1970. Teresa's life story is particularly relevant to her mystical writings; let us therefore review it briefly.

Teresa was born in Avila, Spain, one of ten children from her father Don Alonso's second marriage.[15] Her mother died when she was twelve, and her father, a very pious man, placed her in a school for girls from the nobility run by Augustinian nuns. To her father's chagrin, his favorite daughter became attracted to religious life. Despite his protests, on November 2, 1535 she fled home and entered Avila's Carmelite monastery. Don Alonso finally came to accept this decision.

In 1538, at the age of twenty-three, Teresa became seriously ill. She was in a coma for three days. She somehow was revived, but suffered acute paralysis for three years after this and never fully recovered. Her illness led her to read the bible and some of the classic works of spiritual literature.

As a result, Teresa became exceedingly devoted to prayer. But she admits that after an initial period when she experienced mystical prayer, she had trouble praying until she was thirty-nine. At one point she even briefly abandoned the practice of prayer, thinking that it was the humble thing to do. She later said that this decision was disastrous.

The preceding paragraph recalls what we said in Chapter 4 about the Christian life as process. This is as true of our prayer life as of any other aspect of our spirituality. It is consoling to know that even our most famous contemplatives struggled with prayer. We would do well to recall Teresa's experience when we are going through a dry spell in our own prayer life.[16]

The year 1554 was a turning point for Teresa. The catalysts appear to have been a statue of the suffering Christ that moved her, followed by her reading of Augustine's *Confessions*. Teresa's prayer now regularly took the form of the prayer of quiet, which she describes as a passive form of prayer that flows directly from God into our souls.

Some of her spiritual directors didn't understand Teresa's prayer experiences, and thought she was being seduced by Satan.[17] However, many theologians, teachers, priests, and laypersons were attracted to her spirituality, including the bishop of Avila.

After experiencing a vision of hell, Teresa decided to live a more perfect Carmelite life. In 1562 she founded a new monastery, a small community of eleven nuns. Later she was invited by the general of the Carmelites to found other monasteries, a task she carried out in partnership with John of the Cross. By the time of her death in 1582, Teresa had founded fourteen monasteries. To do this she had to lead quite an active life, which included extensive traveling.

It is noteworthy that Teresa, one of the greatest contemplatives in the history of Christianity, was also heavily involved in service to the church. Her own writings, especially *The Interior Castle*, reflect her concern for keeping these two poles of the Christian life in balance. Let us now take a closer look at this remarkable text.

The castle of which Teresa speaks is really the soul. Teresa wants to describe the movement into the innermost depths of the soul. She speaks of seven dwelling places, the first three of which we can enter through our own spiritual exercises (accompanied, of course, by God's grace). The last four are dwelling places that God deigns to open up to some believers—in these dwelling places the soul passively receives spiritual delights from God.

We should first note that no one is excluded *a priori* from experiencing the favors of the innermost dwelling places. In this respect, the tone of Teresa's writing is much more inclusive than Bernard's. On the other hand, Teresa recognizes that not everyone is going to experience the spiritual delights of the inner rooms. She is very careful to explain that these experiences are not necessary in the life of a Christian. Teresa anticipates this point quite early in *The Interior Castle* when she says to her sisters: "Let us understand, my daughters, that true perfection consists in love of God and neighbor; the more perfectly we keep these two commandments, the more perfect we will be."[18]

Later, when Teresa begins her discussion of the rooms where contemplation begins, she returns to this point. She reminds the sisters that love

> doesn't consist in great delight but in desiring with strong determination to please God in everything, in striving, insofar as possible, not to offend Him, and in asking Him for the advancement of the honor and glory of His Son and the increase of the Catholic Church.[19]

To offer a complete description of the seven dwelling places is beyond the scope of this book. Let us simply highlight some important aspects of the active and passive parts of the castle.

The First Three Dwelling Places

The first three dwelling places represent growth in one's prayer life. The entry to the castle is through prayer and reflection. Teresa acknowledges that even this first stage is difficult for people of good will:

> For even though they are very involved in the world, they have good desires and sometimes, though only once in a while, they entrust themselves to our Lord and reflect on who they are, although in a rather hurried fashion. During the period of a month they will sometimes pray, but their minds are then filled with business matters that ordinarily occupy them. They are so attached to these things that where their treasure lies their heart goes also. Sometimes they do put all these things aside, and the self-knowledge and awareness that they are not proceeding correctly in order to get to the door is important. Finally, they enter

the first, lower rooms. But so many reptiles get in with them that they are prevented from seeing the beauty of the castle and from calming down; they have done quite a bit just by having entered.[20]

Does any of this sound familiar? Have not most of us struggled to enter into the spirit of prayer, finding ourselves distracted by the business (busyness?) of our daily lives? So we find that we only occasionally make time to nurture our relationship with God, and that this time is itself full of distractions. This is a problem that affects full-time ministers and those who have publicly professed a religious life as much as it affects anyone.

Still, Teresa's last point is important: just by entering the castle, however inadequately, we have "done quite a bit." Teresa's gentle affirmations can help us to be more patient with ourselves in our life of prayer.

In the second dwelling places, the soul responds a little more deeply to God's call to prayer, which is heard "through words spoken by other good people, or through sermons, or through what is read in good books," and the like.[21] Notice here how Teresa makes a connection between mysticism and the other two dimensions of the Christian life mentioned by von Hügel, the organizational (i.e., our relationship with others and with the liturgical life of the church) and the intellectual. Even personal prayer does not happen in isolation from others.

Souls who have entered the third dwelling places are those who

long not to offend His Majesty, even guarding themselves against venial sins; they are fond of doing penance and set-ting aside periods for recollection; they spend their time well, practicing works of charity toward their neighbors, and are very balanced in their use of speech and dress and in the governing of their households—those who have them.

Who of us would not be happy to have achieved this level of spiritual perfection? Indeed, Teresa says that "this is a state to be desired," and that souls who have gotten this far will not be denied entrance even into the final dwelling place if they truly desire it.[22]

But even at this stage, there is a danger that we will not persevere. Like the rich man in the gospel (Mt 19:22), we can go away sad when the Lord tells us what we need to do to be perfect. Teresa warns her sisters:

> We seem to think that everything is done when we willingly take and wear the religious habit and abandon all worldly things and possessions for Him....This renunciation is a good enough preparation if one perseveres in it and doesn't turn back and become involved with the vermin in the first rooms, even if it be only in desire.[23]

Teresa addresses this warning to her sisters in community, but it is not hard to see its relevance to Christian spirituality in general. All of us, regardless of our station in life, can become complacent when we reach a certain point in our spiritual growth. We can think that "we have arrived." Furthermore, there is always the danger that we will regress. The spiritual life does not always move forward. Once again, the need for perseverance is clear.

Teresa dwells a little further on this stage, since this one is what brings us to the turning point where we will begin to experience true contemplation. Believers with such "well-ordered lives" may suffer many trials—for example, a loss of wealth or honor, or dryness in prayer. They tend not to see that some of this suffering is due to their own imperfection, specifically a lack of humility.

It is at this stage that Teresa makes a point of the importance of finding a spiritual director. We should not seek someone like ourselves, but "someone who is very free from illusion about the things of the world."[24] Teresa thinks this is necessary if we are to get beyond doing our own will. Notice again Teresa's sensitivity to the communal dimension of the Christian life. We do not attain intimacy with God in isolation from others; rather, we must help one another to grow spiritually.

The Last Four Dwelling Places

I have said more about the first three dwelling places than Teresa does in proportion to the others, because these are the places where I suspect most of us find ourselves most of the time. Perhaps some of us will never experience the kinds of things that Teresa describes in the other dwelling places. Teresa begins her discussion of the fourth dwelling place by saying: "supernatural experiences begin here." These favors are granted by the Lord to "some souls," and Teresa expects that people will enter this dwelling place only after having "had to live in the others a long while."[25]

Earlier, in discussing the first three dwelling places, Teresa makes reference to consolations that God gives to the soul. These are most likely to be experienced in the third dwelling places. Now she moves to a discussion of spiritual delights. What is the difference?

The term "consolations," I think, can be given to those experiences we ourselves acquire through our own meditation and petitions to the Lord, those that proceed from our own nature—although God in the end does have a hand in them; for it must be understood, in whatever I say, that without Him we can do nothing....In sum, joyful consolations in prayer have their beginning in our own human nature and their end in God.

The spiritual delights begin in God, but human nature

feels and enjoys them as much as it does those I mentioned—and much more.[26]

It is worth noting here how careful Teresa is to point out that even our own spiritual exercises are rooted in God, without whom we can do nothing. In the same section, Teresa says of consolations that "it *seems* that we have earned them through our own effort and are rightly consoled for having engaged in such deeds" (emphasis mine). So there is no question here of spiritual exercises like meditation, etc. being "works" by which we lay claim to grace.[27]

Teresa describes spiritual delight, also known as the prayer of quiet, using the analogy of a water trough that fills quietly because the source of the water is within it. She contrasts this with a trough that fills from a complex system of aqueducts. In Teresa's own words:

> The water coming from the aqueducts is comparable, in my opinion, to the consolations I mentioned that are drawn from meditation. For we obtain them through thoughts, assisting ourselves, using creatures to help our meditation, and tiring the intellect. Since, in the end, the consolation comes through our own efforts, noise is made when there has to be some replenishing of the benefits the consolation causes in the soul, as has been said.
>
> With this other fount, the water comes from its own source, which is God.

In what do these spiritual delights consist? Teresa says: "[God] produces this delight with the greatest peace and quiet and sweetness in the very interior part of ourselves." The prayer of quiet, then, is a powerful experience of inner serenity that "begins in God and ends in ourselves."[28]

Teresa acknowledges that sometimes this experience happens serendipitously, "when our Lord is pleased to grant it because He wants to and for no other reason."

However, she recognizes that people will desire to experience the prayer of quiet. The prerequisite, she insists, is *humility*. Paradoxically, we will only obtain these favors if we do not seek them. Why?

> First, because the initial thing necessary for such favors is to love God without self-interest. Second, because there is a slight lack of humility in thinking that for our miserable services something so great can be obtained. Third, because the authentic preparation for these favors on the part of those of us who, after all, have offended Him is the desire to suffer and imitate the Lord rather than to have spiritual delights. Fourth, because His Majesty is not obliged to give them to us as He is to give us glory if we keep His commandments....The fifth reason is that we would be laboring in vain...[this water] is given only to whom God wills to give it and often when the soul is least thinking of it.[29]

Teresa: Detachment with Contemplation

Notice that Teresa puts a different twist on contemplation than Eckhart. Eckhart, as we saw, does not see contemplation as something particularly desirable. Indeed, detachment for Eckhart entails moving beyond any kind of spiritual pleasures. Teresa, on the other hand, sees this kind of contemplative experience as a desirable, although not a necessary or universally experienced, *result* of detachment. What *is* necessary, Teresa never tires of insisting, is that our lives are given over to God in service.

In the remaining dwelling places, Teresa reflects on the experience of union with God. She describes this using the language of the prayer of union, spiritual betrothal (where raptures or ecstasies sometimes take place), and spiritual marriage. We will say more about these things in the next chapter. Basically, the goal is to experience perfect union with God. Interestingly, in the seventh dwelling places, the soul has a fundamentally different experience of God than even in the previous three. Teresa says:

> Now then, when His Majesty is pleased to grant the soul this divine marriage that was mentioned, He first brings it into His own dwelling place. He desires that the favor be different from what it was at other times when He gave the soul raptures. I really believe that in rapture He unites it with Himself, as well as in the prayer of union that was mentioned. But it does not seem to the soul that it is called to enter into its center, as it is here in this dwelling place, but called to the superior part. These things matter little; whether the experience comes in one way or another, the Lord joins the soul to Himself. But He does so by making it blind and deaf, as was Saint Paul in his conversion, and by taking away perception of the nature and kind of favor enjoyed, for the great delight the soul then feels is to see itself near God. Yet when He joins it to Himself, it doesn't understand anything; for all the faculties are lost.[30]

Notice that Teresa refers to this dwelling place as God's own. To emphasize that spiritual delights have been left behind, she uses the analogy of the soul becoming blind and deaf, and unable to grasp or perceive what kind of favors it is receiving. Indeed, Teresa says that "all the faculties are lost" by which we ordinarily apprehend reality. We might say that the state of the soul in Teresa's seventh dwelling places is comparable to Martha's "pure" apprehension of "the One that is God" in Eckhart's sermon.[31] The difference is that Teresa sees the other stages of contemplation as desirable, while Eckhart does not.

The Fruits of Contemplative Prayer

But let us move to the *pièce de résistance* of Teresa's narrative: what she says about the *effects* of contemplative prayer. Teresa lists many, but one that stands out is "forgetfulness of self." Teresa says: "There is a great detachment from everything and a desire to be always either alone or occupied in something that will benefit some soul."[32] She goes on to talk about the *purpose* of God's favors, speaking with great passion:

O my sisters! How forgetful this soul, in which the Lord dwells in so particular a way, should be of its own rest, how little it should care for its honor, and how far it should be from wanting esteem in anything! For if it is with Him very much, as is right, it should think little about itself. All its concern is taken up with how to please Him more and how or where it will show Him the love it bears Him. *This is the reason for prayer, my daughters, the purpose of this spiritual marriage: the birth always of good works, good works.*[33]

We have already seen that Teresa is consistent in hammering away at this point throughout her description of the dwelling places. She goes on to make an even more clear and emphatic statement:

I repeat, it is necessary that your foundation consist of more than prayer and contemplation. If you do not strive for the virtues and practice them, you will always be dwarfs. And, please God, it will be only a matter of not growing, for you already know that whoever does not increase decreases. I hold that love, where present, cannot possibly be content with remaining always the same.[34]

We should mark carefully here Teresa's insistence on the Christian life as process, a theme that goes hand in hand with action and contemplation.

Teresa also reminds her readers that the path she is proposing is the same one trod by other believers. She refers to the Martha and Mary story to underline her point:

> It would indeed be novel to think of having these favors from God through a path other than the one He took and the one followed by all His saints. May the thought never enter our minds. Believe me, Martha and Mary must join together in order to show hospitality to the Lord and have Him always present and not host Him badly by failing to give Him something to eat. How would Mary, always seated at His feet, provide Him with food if her sister did not help her? His food is that in every way possible we draw souls that they may be saved and praise him always.[35]

Unlike Eckhart, Teresa says that we must be *both* Martha and Mary to have a healthy spirituality. It is not a question of having to choose either an active or a contemplative life.

To those who object that they are unable to bring souls to God, Teresa responds that God is not asking them to do the impossible: "You need not be desiring to benefit the whole world but must concentrate on those who are in your company."[36] This is important news for us today. Now more than ever, we are aware of the massive problems of the whole world, not just of our immediate environment. Today we *must* think and act globally in a way that Teresa could never have imagined—the survival of the human race is at stake. Still, it remains true that none of us can save the world. We can make a difference by serving those "in our company," even as we strive in small ways to serve those we cannot see, for example, by contributing time and/or money to organizations that try to feed the hungry or secure justice for the oppressed.[37] A final remark by Teresa is worth quoting in this connection: "The Lord doesn't look so much at the greatness of our works as at the love with which they are done."[38]

Finding the Balance

There has been a tendency in much literature about mysticism to identify it with contemplation; but contemplation is only one side of mysticism, albeit an important one. We have looked at three mystics who grappled with the question of balancing the active and contemplative dimensions of the spiritual life. Of the three, Bernard expresses a certain bias against the active life (at least theoretically if not in practice), Eckhart expresses a bias against the contemplative life, and Teresa sees both in a positive light. We should not be disturbed by the differences here. They undoubtedly relate to each author's personality, environment, and experiences.

The balance, indeed, is going to be a little different for each of us. It is not necessarily a question of counting the number of hours that we pray vs. the number of hours that we spend in service of others. The point is that we need to find room for both dimensions of the spiritual life, and periodically evaluate where we stand.

There are some people in the world who dedicate the greater part of their lives to contemplation. It is interesting to hear people's reactions to this phenomenon, e.g., as manifested in groups that take vows of silence or that remain cloistered in a monastery or convent. Most people seem to think that this is a waste of one's life or an unhealthy spirituality. But we should remember that for these groups, prayer is a form of activity performed on behalf of the world. When we look at how far the world is from the reign of God, perhaps we should be grateful that some people have dedicated their whole lives to prayer on its behalf! We should also remember that there are other active dimensions of the lives of these communities.

For most of us, as was mentioned previously, the opposite emphasis usually prevails. Our lives are active and busy, and we find it hard to devote sufficient time and energy to nourishing our inner life with God. But, as I hope this chapter has made clear, it is very important that we do so. John Tauler, in one of his sermons, makes this point with particular poignancy:

> Whatever a man does, whatever exterior works he undertakes, he should never allow himself to forget the life in the center of his soul, and should do everything in his power to keep his attention firmly fixed there. If only he will do this, he can perform as many active works as he pleases, without ever disturbing his true peace; but if he forsakes the depths of his soul, he will find no peace in active works, because all his outward activity will be inspired by folly. Being moved by his senses and unduly intent upon external affairs, he will be deaf to the voice of God, inspiring and warning him in his soul.[39]

Love of God and Love of Neighbor

Finally, let us say a word about love of God and neighbor. Although Bernard sometimes connects contemplation with love of God and action with love of neighbor, the two are really intertwined. Contemporary Christian theologians stress that the two kinds of love should be seen as two sides to the same coin, i.e., love of neighbor is a manifestation of love of God. Bernard's argument certainly recognizes this, as we saw. In our own day, with its emphasis on our Christian responsibility to promote social justice, we are perhaps more sensitive to stressing this connection.[40]

We are certainly on solid ground here, as the New Testament often makes this precise point. In Matthew's sermon on the mount, Jesus declares: "Not everyone who says to me, 'Lord, Lord,' will enter the kingdom of heaven, but only the one who does the will of my Father in heaven" (Mt 7:21). Later in the gospel, Jesus makes a clear identification between doing God's will and serving our sisters and brothers in need:

> For I was hungry and you gave me food, I was thirsty and you gave me something to drink, I was a stranger and you welcomed me, I was naked and you gave me clothing, I was sick and you took care of me, I was in prison and you visited me.

When the righteous in turn ask Jesus, "Lord, when did we do any of these things for you?" the Lord responds with a chilling reminder: "Truly I tell you, just as you did it to one of the least of these who are members of my family, you did it to me" (Mt 25:35–40).

Similarly, in the first letter of John, we hear: "Those who say, 'I love God,' and hate their brothers or sisters, are liars; for those who do not love a brother or sister whom they have seen, cannot love God whom they have not seen" (1 Jn 4:20).

The active dimension of our spirituality is what keeps us connected with the community of faith, even as it expresses our love for God. As long as it is nurtured, we need not worry about the danger of our own mysticism "centering in an 'I' and ending in schism."

6

Union with God

Chapter 2 mentioned the famous *Baltimore Catechism* that was the centerpiece of religious education for many older Roman Catholics. In its very first chapter, the catechism posed the question: "Why did God make me?" The answer was clear and succinct: "God made me to know, love, and serve him in this world and to be happy with him in heaven."

Today when we ask the question "What is the meaning and purpose of life?" we wish that there was such a clear, simple, and reliable answer. The world seems so complicated now, and the catechism's answer—while most Christians still believe it in some form or another—sounds naive and simplistic as it stands.

The medieval mystics usually answer the question about the meaning and purpose of life in terms of some kind of "union with God." They rarely give a short or simple account of what this expression means. On the contrary, they think that this sublime goal of the spiritual life is worthy of extended and carefully nuanced discussion. This chapter will describe the basic notions of mystical union that predominated during the medieval period, and offer some reflections about their significance for today.

This theme, in a sense, ties together all of the others we have examined. For to be united with God means coming to know God experientially, accepting the dynamic of divine-human activity, persevering through the ups and downs of the spiritual life, and balancing life's active and contemplative dimensions.

Two understandings of mystical union were prominent during the late middle ages: (1) a "relational" union, described in such terms as a union of wills or spirits, or as a union in love, and (2) an "essential" union, described in such terms as "absorption" into God or "identity" with God. This approach is sometimes described as "intellectual" because it develops some of the ideas of so-called neo-Platonic philosophy.

It would be better to speak of these two approaches as tendencies or emphases, because often they both appear in a single mystic's writings, and, as we shall see, they are not mutually exclusive. Let us look first at relational union.

Relational Union: A Union in Love

This conception of union is dominant in mystics like Bernard of Clairvaux, Francis of Assisi, and Teresa of Avila. It is also the kind of union that is described in classic Protestant texts from the reformation period (sixteenth century). We will be looking at John Calvin's understanding of union as an example.

Let us begin with Bernard of Clairvaux. We already saw that Bernard speaks of stages of loving God. At the third stage, "loving God for God's sake," Bernard speaks of a kind of "state of union" wherein our wills are so conformed to God's that we will have no trouble loving our neighbor. The ultimate union with God only happens when we reach the fourth stage, "loving even ourselves for God's sake." Bernard expects that this will take place for most people after their deaths, and indeed only after the final resurrection. However, he does concede that some people have occasional fleeting experiences of such union during their earthly life.

Bernard describes the experience of union at the fourth stage of loving God as follows:

> It is therefore necessary for our souls to reach a similar state in which, just as God willed everything to exist for himself, so we wish that neither ourselves nor other beings to have been nor to be except for his will alone; not for our pleasure....It is deifying to go through such an experience. As a drop of water seems to disappear completely in a big quantity of wine, even assuming the wine's taste and color; just as red, molten iron becomes so much like fire it seems to lose its primary state; just as the air on a sunny day seems transformed into sunshine instead of being lit up; so it is necessary for the saints that all human feelings melt in a mysterious way and flow into the will of God. Otherwise, how could God be all in all if something human survives in man? No doubt, the substance remains though under another form, another glory, another power.[1]

Several things are noteworthy about this passage. First, Bernard presents here several of the most famous images of mystical union that have come down to us through the ages: the drop of water merging into the vat of wine, the iron taking on the qualities of fire, etc. These images suggest a kind of "absorption" into God. But Bernard is very careful in his use of language. A distinguished Bernard scholar, Etienne Gilson, has this to say about the passage quoted above:

> The drop of water? "Deficere a se tota *videtur*" [it seems to disappear completely]; it seems to have, but we know well that it has not, ceased to exist, even if it is infinitely diluted. The inflamed iron? "Igni *simillimum* fit" [it becomes so

much like fire...]; it becomes as similar to fire as possible, but it does not become fire, indeed, it must not become fire, in order that it may become like it. The air illuminated by the sun? It so absorbs its light, "ut non tam illuminatus, quam ipsum lumen esse *videatur*" [it seems transformed into sunshine, instead of being lit up]. Here again, it is only an appearance, the transfiguration of an indestructible substance into the glorious form that it would henceforth display. Thus, St. Bernard never spoke of an annihilation of the creature, but of a transformation.[2]

Indeed, Bernard makes it clear that the substance of the soul remains, but it is transformed, i.e., "under another form, another glory, another power."

Another thing to notice is how Bernard speaks of everything flowing into the will of God. Bernard's union in love is therefore a union of wills. The more we love God, the more we want to do God's will in all things. We can also call this a "spiritual" union (as opposed to a "substantive" one). Indeed, Bernard often refers to 1 Corinthians 6:17 to describe mystical union. There Paul says: "Anyone united to the Lord becomes one spirit with him."

Here we might wish to recall the definition by Jean Gerson cited in Chapter 1, for Bernard's understanding corresponds to it very closely:

Mystical theology is experiential knowledge of God attained through the union of spiritual affection with him. Through this union the words of the Apostle are fulfilled: "He who clings to God is one spirit with Him (1 Cor 6:17)."[3]

However, Bernard and others who spoke in this fashion did not simply leave it at that. They looked for images to describe this union. One image that was quite common was that of the spiritual marriage, where the soul was described as the bride and Jesus as the bridegroom. This image did not come out of a hat; it had its roots in the allegorical interpretation of the biblical book, the Song of Songs.

Most biblical scholars today regard the Song of Songs as a poem celebrating human love, but it may have been included in the Jewish bible because it was taken as an allegory of God's love for the people of Israel. The medieval mystics literally had a field day with this text. Bernard himself wrote eighty-six sermons on the Song of Songs, and never made it past the second chapter of the book.

In Sermon 83 on the Song, Bernard says:

> When she loves perfectly, the soul is wedded to the Word. What is lovelier than this conformity? What is more desirable than charity, by whose operation, O soul, not content with a human master, you approach the Word with confidence, cling to him with constancy, speak to him as to a familiar friend, and refer to him in every matter with an intellectual grasp proportionate to the boldness of your desire? Truly this is a spiritual contract, a holy marriage. It is more than a contract, it is an embrace: an embrace where identity of will makes of two one spirit.[4]

Notice again how Bernard describes union with God in terms of perfect love, and how he returns to the notion of "one spirit." Notice too how for Bernard, there is a *knowledge* of God that corresponds to this perfect love. This recalls our discussion of love and knowledge in Chapter 2.[5]

As we saw in the last chapter, Teresa of Avila also used the image of the spiritual marriage. Teresa distinguishes between the spiritual betrothal, which takes place in the sixth dwelling places, and the spiritual marriage, which takes place in the seventh. Spiritual betrothal (analogous to the engagement of a married couple) is characterized by raptures or visions, which Teresa describes in some detail.[6]

She sees this stage as one where the soul gets in touch with its "superior part," whereas in the spiritual marriage it is "called to enter into its center."[7]

Teresa sees a great difference between the two dwelling places. In the spiritual marriage,

> The Lord appears in this center of the soul, not in an imaginative vision but in an intellectual one, although more delicate than those mentioned, as He appeared to the apostles without entering through the door when He said to them *pax vobis*. What God communicates here to the soul in an instant is a secret so great and a favor so sublime—and the delight the soul experiences so extreme—that I don't know what to compare it to. I can say only that the Lord wishes to reveal for that moment, in a more sublime manner than through any spiritual vision or taste, the glory of heaven. One can say no more—insofar as can be understood—than that the soul, I mean the spirit, is made one with God.[8]

In language reminiscent of Eckhart, Teresa goes on to say that "it is very certain that in emptying ourselves of all that is creature and detaching ourselves from it for the love of God, the same Lord will fill us with Himself."[9]

Significantly, Teresa describes the experience of union in terms of God and the soul rejoicing together "in the deepest silence." She does not speak of the faculties being suspended, however. "In my opinion," she says, "the faculties are not lost here; they do not work, but remain as though in amazement."[10]

Teresa does seem to think that the soul that arrives in this dwelling place will stay there. However, this does not mean that it sees no possibility of falling. Indeed, the soul now becomes even more vigilant and fearful of any offense against God.[11] On the positive side, in this dwelling place "there are almost never any experiences of dryness or interior disturbance of the kind that was present at times in all the other dwelling places, but the soul is almost always in quiet."[12]

In no place does Teresa suggest that the soul becomes absorbed into God. Hers is clearly a relational concept of union—indeed, Teresa makes reference to Paul's statement in 1 Corinthians 6 to describe the spiritual marriage.[13]

However carefully the language of union may have been expressed by mystics like Bernard and Teresa, it has not been without its critics. In particular, Protestant commentators have often rejected mysticism on the grounds that it obliterates the distinction between God and ourselves, a distinction that will always exist because of our status as sinful creatures. For example, the nineteenth century theologian Albrecht Ritschl rejected Bernard's love-mysticism on this ground:

> For love very distinctly implies the equality of the person loving with the beloved. St. Bernard, who gave to the world the pattern of this species of piety, expressly states that in intercourse with the Bridegroom awe ceases, majesty is laid aside, and immediate personal intercourse is carried on as between lovers or neighbors.

In contrast, according to Ritschl, the reformers shifted to faith, which "denies the possibility of equality" with God.[14]

However, a close look at Bernard's writings shows that Bernard clearly does not speak of a union of equals. He expressly states that the relationship is one in which God condescends to share love with us,[15] and that there is no question of a "betrothal or union of equals."[16] What Bernard *does* claim is that there is a perfectly *mutual* relationship between the Bride and the Bridegroom. In one of Bernard's *Sermons on the Song of Songs*, he clearly distinguishes between mutuality and equality:

> Although the creature *loves less*, being a *lesser being*, yet if it
> loves with its whole heart nothing is lacking, for it has given
> all....For it is nothing other than love, holy and chaste, full
> of sweetness and delight, love utterly serene and true, *mutu-*
> *al* and deep, which joins two beings, not in one flesh, but
> in one spirit, making them no longer two but one.[17]

Ritschl's analysis of Bernard's mysticism thus suffers from
an inadequate reading of the texts.

In our own century, most people have come to recognize that the criticism of mysticism in earlier Protestant
sources needs to be reassessed. Since the Second Vatican
Council in the 1960s, Roman Catholics and Protestants
have moved to a new level of respect for and dialogue with
one another. There is a recognition that what we took
before as irreconcilable conflicts are often matters of
emphasis. Thus we do not need to pit Catholic "mystical"
spirituality against Protestant "faith-centered" spirituality.
The two approaches really complement one another when
properly understood. In fact, scholars now speak openly of
a spirituality in classic reformers like Luther and Calvin.
This book will use John Calvin's understanding of union
with Christ as an example of Protestant mystical theology.

It is interesting that Bernard of Clairvaux does not use
the term "mystical union" in describing union with God.
Calvin, on the other hand, *does* use the term on a few occa-
sions. The most famous occurrence is in the following passage from the *Institutes*:

> Therefore, that joining together of Head and members,
> that indwelling of Christ in our hearts—in short, that mysti-
> cal union—are accorded by us the highest degree of impor-
> tance, so that Christ, having been made ours, makes us
> sharers with him in the gifts with which he has been
> endowed. We do not, therefore, contemplate him outside
> ourselves from afar in order that his righteousness may be

imputed to us but because we put on Christ and are engrafted into his body—in short, because he deigns to make us one with him. For this reason, we glory that we have fellowship of righteousness with him.[18]

To whom is this experience of mystical union granted? For Calvin, the answer is simple: it is granted to all of the elect, that is, to all those who are predestined to receive the gift of faith.[19] The way this happens is that the Holy Spirit brings the elect to faith through the hearing of the gospel; in so doing, the Spirit "engrafts" them into Christ. Thus, mystical union is a direct result of faith. To put it in Calvin's own words: "Christ, when he illumines us into faith by the power of his Spirit, at the same time so engrafts us into his body that we become partakers of every good."[20]

Engrafting, a word that appears in both of the last two quotations, is one of Calvin's favorite images for describing union with Christ. Just as Bernard often quotes 1 Corinthians 6:17 (the "one spirit" text), Calvin often uses Ephesians 5:29 in describing mystical union, i.e., that we become "flesh of God's flesh, bone of God's bone."[21] Calvin is clear that he is referring to a real and not a figurative union:

Christ is not outside us but dwells within us. Not only does he cleave to us by an indivisible bond of fellowship, but with a wonderful communion, day by day, he grows more and more into one body with us, until he becomes completely one with us.[22]

However, Calvin makes it equally clear that he is not referring to any kind of absorption into God. Our union with Christ is real and intimate, but spiritual. In fact, one of his constant refrains when discussing union with Christ is that it happens in the power of the Holy Spirit:

Such is the union between us and Christ, that *in a sense* He pours Himself into us. For we are not bone of His bone, and flesh of His flesh, because, like ourselves, He is man, but because, *by the power of His Spirit,* He engrafts us into His Body, so that from Him we derive life.[23]

When he considers the question of the nature of mystical union, Calvin's language becomes very tentative. In a letter to one of his contemporaries, Calvin says: "How this happens far exceeds the limits of my understanding, I must confess; thus I have more of an impression of this mystery than I strive to comprehend it."[24] The only thing of which he is sure is that the power of the Holy Spirit flows from heaven to earth.[25]

Perhaps more important is what Calvin thinks are the *effects* of this union. In this respect he is similar to Bernard and Teresa. Calvin thinks that union with Christ through faith will spill over into a life that is dedicated to the love of God and of other people. He expresses this succinctly in the *Institutes*: "First, indeed, our soul should be entirely filled with the love of God. From this will flow directly the love of neighbor."[26] This quotation shows that Calvin, like Bernard, believes that, strictly speaking, the love of God takes priority over the love of other people, as we saw in the last chapter.[27] But it is really not a question of pitting one against the other. Indeed, Calvin goes on to say that "our life shall best conform to God's will and the prescription of the law when it is in every respect most fruitful for our brethren."[28] (Note here the stress on a union of wills, similar to Bernard's conception.) Thus, union with Christ is not an end in itself—it becomes the basis of our giving glory to God in active lives of service. As Calvin puts it, "We must at all times seek after love and look toward the edification of our neighbor."[29]

There are certainly some significant differences between

Calvin's conception of mystical union and the typical medieval conception. For example, Calvin has practically no interest in contemplation, unlike Bernard and Teresa. Still, we can say that the basic goal of union is the same: to be spiritually united with God.

Essential Union

This conception of mystical union tends to speak of an identity or loss of distinction between God and the believer. It has already been noted that this conception is the one that has traditionally been sharply criticized by Protestant commentators. In fact, Protestantism was not alone in being suspicious of it—the Catholic Church also challenged some of the formulations proposed by mystics of this strain. Many authors who are hostile to mysticism tend to assume that this is the kind of union that mystics always mean when they write about union with God. These authors also tend to oversimplify and hence to misunderstand what the mystics are saying, often through a highly selective reading of mystical texts.

That being said, let us look more closely at this notion of union. We begin with Meister Eckhart, one of those who got into trouble for some of his writings.[30]

Eckhart was actually quite comfortable using the kind of language and imagery that we saw in Bernard and Teresa. For example, in one of his Counsels on Discernment, Eckhart is emphatic that what we should seek from God is "what is his very dearest will":

> This is what God looks for in all things, that we surrender our will....Truly, without giving up our own will in all things, we never accomplish anything in God's sight. But if it were to progress so far that we gave up the whole of our will and had the courage to renounce everything, external

and internal, for the love of God, then we would have accomplished all things, and not until then."[31]

In another Counsel on Discernment, Eckhart speaks about the body of the Lord (eucharist). He notes as one of the conditions of approaching the table: "that [one's] will be turned to God, that he intends nothing and delights in nothing except in God and what is wholly godly, and that everything should displease him that is unlike God."[32] Later in the same section, he proceeds to expound the image of the drop of water in a cask of wine. At least in this passage, he is careful to point out that a distinction remains between God and the soul:

> This union is far closer than if one were to pour a drop of water into a cask of wine; there, we still have water and wine, but here we have such a changing into one that there is no creature who can find the distinction.[33]

Here we find much that is familiar to Bernard: the notion of *unus spiritus* (in the sense of a union of wills)[34] and the use of a common medieval image for union (water in the vat of wine).[35]

Eckhart also uses other imagery that is reminiscent of Bernard's, particularly bridal imagery. For example, in one of his German sermons, Eckhart says: "When God created the soul, he created it according to his highest perfection, so that it might be a bride of the Only-Begotten Son."[36]

Although Eckhart at times uses language that is suggestive of Bernard and the other love-mystics, he is willing to go further than they are in his language of union. Eckhart was willing to use *both* the language of "one spirit" and "one substance."[37] Thus, throughout his works, "Eckhart insists upon the absolute oneness of God and the soul."[38]

To give but a few examples, in one of his sermons (where Eckhart reflects on the text of Wisdom 5:16, "The just will live forever"), Eckhart declares: "What is life? God's being is my life. If my life is God's being, then God's existence must be my existence and God's is-ness is my is-ness, neither less nor more."[39] Later in the same sermon, he says: "What is changed into something else becomes one with it. I am so changed into him that he produces his being in me as one, not just similar. By the living God, this is true! There is no distinction."[40] Similarly, in another sermon Eckhart speaks of encountering God "without a medium."[41]

This kind of language is of course problematic for a *Christian* understanding of mysticism, as we saw in Chapter 1. Christian mysticism, Jerald Brauer reminds us, "always has some relation to the person of Christ, the reality of the Church, the Christian ethic, and the Christian sacraments."[42] Recall, too, von Hügel's aversion to what he called "pure mysticism,"[43] which neglects the other dimensions of the Christian life.

It was precisely for statements like these that Eckhart was cited for heresy. Can he be defended against the charges? Recent studies have suggested that passages that speak of absolute oneness, when seen in the full context of Eckhart's thought, preserve "the difference in identity that other mystics have expressed in less daring ways."[44] A growing number of authors today thus suspect that the medieval condemnation of certain of Eckhart's ideas was "at least in part unsound."[45]

Much of the contemporary defense of Eckhart centers around the proper understanding of his *in quantum* principle. Put simply, this principle states that whatever identity the soul has with God, it does not have this identity of itself, but only *insofar as it is touched by God's grace*. Indeed, Eckhart thinks that our very being is grounded in the reality of God. As he puts it in one of his scripture commentaries, "Everything except God possesses existence from some-

thing else and from somewhere else."[46] Theologian John
Caputo provides an enlightening explanation of this:

> Creatures are nothing apart from their relationship to God,
> for nothing can be except by being, as white things are
> white by whiteness itself. But being is God. [Eckhart] meant
> to stress the radical dependence of creatures upon God.
> But more importantly he meant to say that creatures are
> but shadows and likenesses of being itself. They do not
> "have" being, but their being is "lent," borrowed, image-
> like, even as the truly poor in spirit "have nothing."...
> Creatures have being because they are related to God who
> *is* being.[47]

Thus it is not correct to say that Eckhart speaks in an
unqualified way of an identity between God and the
graced soul.

You may recall from the last chapter that Eckhart,
despite his daring language of identity with God, was not
terribly interested in the contemplative life. He saw this
identity with God as playing itself out in ordinary consciousness and in ordinary everyday activities.[48] We saw this
illustrated in his unique interpretation of the Martha and
Mary story. Martha was aware that her being was totally in
God, and she was therefore in Eckhart's eyes totally free to
be of service, while Mary was still searching for a contemplative experience.

John Tauler, one of Eckhart's disciples, also spoke frequently in his writings about mystical union. Well aware
of the condemnation of some of his master's ideas, he
was generally much more careful in expounding the
meaning of this union. This is not to say that he wasn't
willing to play with the language of identity. Consider, for
example, this description of union with God in one of his
sermons:

The soul escapes from itself and from all created things, for in the simplicity of God it casts off all multiplicity, transcending it completely. The higher faculties of the soul are raised up into heaven where God's holiness dwells in unity. There they find their happiness and true joy in God....In this state a man can lose himself in God. Nothing remains for him but to praise the Lord for all the wonderful and particular gifts which He has showered upon him, for he sees that they are all in God's hands and does not attribute them to himself.[49]

At times, Tauler uses stronger language than this, more reminiscent of Eckhart himself. In a sermon where he speaks of both a similarity and a dissimilarity between God and the soul, he goes on to speak of a higher stage:

In this conversion, the purified and clarified spirit sinks completely into the divine darkness, into a still silence and an inconceivable and inexpressible unity. In this absorption all like and unlike is lost. In this abyss the spirit loses itself and knows neither God nor itself, neither like nor unlike. It knows nothing, for it is engulfed in the oneness of God and has lost all differences.[50]

However, in other passages he speaks of the soul losing all *sense* of distinction, but not *in fact* losing distinction:

Then the soul is led still further on, into a unity which is God's oneness, simple, without recognizable marks, so that the soul loses all sense of difference between God and itself. I do not say that all difference between God and the soul disappears, but that the soul loses its sense of difference, because in unity all multiplicity is lost, and it is unity which unifies diversity.[51]

Basically, Tauler follows Eckhart in his use of the *in quantum* principle. In another passage on mystical union, he describes the nature of the union as follows:

> Here the soul becomes completely God-colored, divine and godly. It becomes everything by grace that God is by nature in the union with God, in the absorption in God. It is held above itself in God. Thus, it becomes God-colored there. Should it then see itself, it would see itself completely as God. And whoever should see it would see it in the clothes, color, manner, and being of God by grace. And who so sees would be blessed in his beholding, for God and the soul are one in this union by grace, not by nature.[52]

Here we see Tauler explicitly speaking of a unity by grace and not by nature. Reflecting on this distinction, the German theologian Heinrich Denifle said: "What does this mean? It means nothing else but that the soul does not become God naturally and *essentially*, but rather through participation....For if they are *essentially* one, then the soul is 'naturally' God, and not God 'by grace.'"[53]

Obviously, the notion of union as developed by Eckhart and Tauler would be problematic for many Christians. Even if we give them the benefit of the doubt and acknowledge that they did not intend to speak in an unqualified way of identity with God, their language does sometimes seem to imply a closeness to God that borders on the blasphemous. On the other hand, we must remember that Tauler and Eckhart were most interested in an awareness of unity with God that was expressed in lives of virtue and service.

Union with Christ Today

This chapter, perhaps more so than the others in this book, speaks of things that can seem very far removed from our everyday experience. This is because mystical union is for most people a rather esoteric concept. Perhaps the most down to earth expression of it is provided by John Calvin, who simply sees it as a fact of Christian existence, an immediate result of faith that in turn prompts us to serve God and one another in love. This relational conception of union stands in the tradition of such Catholic authors as Bernard and Teresa.

For most Christians most of the time, this seems to be the kind of union that happens for them. All of us want to be in a good *relationship* with God. We generally experience God as other and wish to be united with God's will by living according to God's commandments.

In practical terms, mystical union has to do with experiencing God's presence in our lives in an intimate way. God is *always* present to us; to use Augustine's famous phrase, God is closer to us than we are to ourselves. Sometimes, though, our lives are such that we are distracted from our awareness of this. This is why it is so important to cultivate a life of prayer, both personal and communal. If we make it a point to "tune in" regularly to God's presence, perhaps that presence will become more obvious to us in our other daily activities.

Although few may be privileged to have the kind of intense contemplative experience that is described by Bernard and Teresa, I believe that most of us do have peak experiences that have a certain mystical quality. When my friends talk about experiencing the birth of their children, they use language that sounds very mystical. Even friends whom I would not describe as particularly religious will speak of being spiritually uplifted and awe-struck at the miracle of birth.

Painful or tragic experiences can also have this effect. A few years ago, I was involved in a life-threatening situation in which a student was bleeding severely. Those of us who were present had to act fast. While applying direct pressure to the wound, we managed to get the student to the college infirmary, where an ambulance would meet us.

When the professionals finally took over, I went to wash my hands, which were covered with blood. A few of us then went to the emergency room with the student and stayed by his side while he was being treated. It was a terrifying experience, but I was also uplifted by the teamwork, support, and concern that were shown by so many people that night.

A few days later, I was presiding at a mass in the college chapel. During the consecration, when I spoke the words, "This is my body," my thoughts rushed to the broken body of that student two nights before. When I pronounced the words, "This is my blood," I looked into the chalice and thought of his blood. In that instant, the full meaning of the eucharist hit me with an impact that I cannot even now put into words. But I now *felt* what I had always *believed*: the connection between the body of Christ that is the eucharist and the body of Christ that is the church. It was an emotional experience, fleeting but powerful. If ever I felt as though I was in union with God, it was at that moment.

Perhaps we have all had these experiences more often than we realize, and just don't have the words to describe them. Or maybe we're afraid to name an experience as mystical for fear of being labeled a kook or taken away by people in white coats. (This is not to say that mystics are never kooks—some have been!) It is unfortunate that in our society we have so often suppressed or denied the spiritual dimension that is present in all of us.

It is especially important that we recognize the connection between union with God and with one another. For Christians, there can be no other way. We must always remember Jesus' words, that as often as we do good things for the least of his brothers and sisters, we do them for him (Mt 25:40). Contemplation and action must always go hand in hand.

To speak of mystical experience, then, is to speak of intimacy with God. Every believer longs for this. We can get caught up in arguments about the meaning of mystical union—indeed, the material presented in this chapter only scratches the surface of the issue—but in the end, the experience of God cannot be contained in arguments. It is something that only the heart can understand.

Epilogue

Most of this book was written in Germany, where I enjoyed the warm hospitality of the German Franciscans for a sabbatical semester and two summers. As we sat in the recreation room one evening, a German friar who has an interest in mysticism told me that his reading of Meister Eckhart had led him to a new image of God. He spoke of Eckhart's writings opening the door to a wider understanding of his faith.

This friar is not a professor at a university; he is not a priest; in fact, he has not, so far as I know, studied theology in any formal program. But he is a person who is deeply concerned about the spiritual life, and I think it is significant that his reading of mystical literature has had such a deep effect on his spiritual development.

That is, finally, why I wrote this book. To me, the mystics are attractive not only because of their unique and fascinating perspectives on theology, but because they can help us to move to a more mature outlook on our faith and a more mature response to its challenges. This kind of growing up in the faith needs to happen in all of our lives, not just the lives of professionally religious people like theologians, pastors, and members of religious orders.

Some Christians might object that we need nothing beyond the sacred scriptures to nurture our spiritual lives.

Here I must gently but firmly disagree, for two reasons. First, the mystics themselves are deeply immersed in scripture, and indeed base most of their ideas on scriptural texts. To be sure, they sometimes have an unconventional way of interpreting the Bible! But their love of and rootedness in scripture is one of their strongest assets. Many authors have pointed to the mystical dimension in the scriptures themselves, as I have tried to do in a general way in the chapters of this book. The mystics didn't invent this dimension; rather, they recognized it and reflected on its significance. There is no intrinsic opposition between an evangelical (scripture-based) and a mystical spirituality.

Second, to claim that scripture is the sole source of authority in Christianity is to do an injustice both to scripture and to the other ways in which God's presence and activity are manifest in the world. Some Christians treat the scriptures as if they simply fell one day from the sky, complete with leather binding, gilded edges, and the words of Jesus in red. We must remember that the scriptures were written centuries ago in a culture vastly different from our own, and that most of us are not reading the scriptures directly but in translation. There is indeed a divine inspiration to the Bible that makes it timeless, but the sense in which this is true can only be discerned when one also understands its historical and literary dimensions. To refuse this task is to refuse to accept the Bible on its own terms.

One might even say that the scriptures are largely a product of mystical experience, conceived in its broadest sense as an intuition of the presence of God in creation and in human history. They are the record of the Jewish and Christian experience of divine revelation. To be sure, the scriptures can help us to unpack the meaning of this world in which we live. But we need to pay attention to other ways in which that meaning is revealed to us: through personal experience, through scientific experiments, etc. Revelation cannot be confined to the bible.

Nor can revelation or mysticism be confined to the experience of Christians. While this book has dealt exclusively with Christian mysticism, it must be remembered that other religious traditions also are the bearers of genuine religious insights and experiences. Every known religion has a mystical dimension, and Christians can only benefit from acquainting themselves with some of the riches that are found in other religious communities. The twentieth century mystic Thomas Merton is an outstanding example of how fruitful such a dialogue with other traditions can be.

David Tracy, a distinguished Roman Catholic theologian, is fond of talking about two basic forms of religious expression: manifestation and proclamation. Manifestation has to do with an experience of participating in the transcendent. Celebrations of the sacraments (at least in the understanding of many Christian denominations) would be included here. For example, Catholics and many other Christians believe that in receiving communion, they experience a genuine encounter with the living God. Proclamation, on the other hand, has to do with an experience of the transcendent as other, of God as radically different from us and to whom we must submit. Thus, the prophets proclaim a God who stands apart from us and challenges us.[1]

It is easy to associate manifestation with mystics, who stress union with God, and to associate proclamation with evangelicals, who stress the preached word that calls us to conversion. But in truth, these two religious expressions must go together as two sides to the same coin.

The mystics are indeed a good example of manifestation in their experiences of God as intimately present to them and to other believers. But there is also a sense in which the mystics are prophetic, in that they recognize a gap between ourselves and God, a gap that will never be completely bridged. Even the mystics who speak of a kind of unity of identity are well aware of this.

The mystics are uniquely prophetic for our day, in that they offer us an alternative vision of the Christian life. If this is a threat to institutional religion, then it is a healthy and a necessary one. To be sure, mystically-inclined Christians must be careful not to substitute a tyranny of personal experience for a tyranny of centralized authority. The well-balanced Christian recognizes that there is a need for both personal experience and structures of authority, as well as for the speculative dimension, as von Hügel so rightly insists.

As a theologian, I am amazed that many of the insights of the medieval mystics are so relevant to current theological issues. For example, the chapter on knowledge of God suggested ways in which the mystics can contribute to the present-day discussion about God-language. Similarly, the chapter on grace and freedom focused on the mystics' insights into human responsibility, a theme that is strongly stressed in present-day ecological and "nuclear age" theologies.

If this book has helped the reader to grow in her or his faith in even the smallest way, then it has achieved its purpose. I mentioned in Chapter 1 that this book is a primer, and I sincerely hope that the reader will have been inspired to read further in the writings of one or more of the mystics, including others who are not presented here. For all the mystics that this book has introduced, they are only a few representatives of a much broader phenomenon embracing scores of men and women down through the ages. To help those readers who wish to pursue further their interest in mysticism, I have appended a list of suggested readings, including some secondary sources (writings about rather than by the mystics) that might be of interest.

But let us never be content just with reading the mystics. Mysticism—as intimacy with God—is ultimately something to be lived, not just studied. Our goal—which each of us will approach in a different way—is to respond to the gift of divine grace and so to become one spirit with God.

Notes

1. What Is Mysticism?

1. *New Catholic Encyclopedia*, 1967 ed., s.v. "Mysticism," by T. Corbishley, vol. 10, p. 175.

2. Evelyn Underhill, *Mysticism* (New York: E. P. Dutton and Co., 1961), p. xii.

3. I am referring here to an aversion to mysticism that has been characteristic of Protestant thought. Specifically, mysticism is associated with "Catholic" works-righteousness (since mystics are often known for engaging in special disciplines of prayer or Christian service) and is set in opposition to "Protestant" faith. Thankfully, this caricature of mysticism has been challenged in recent scholarly literature. There is a strong mystical element in much classic Protestant literature, including the works of Luther and Calvin, and it is not in opposition to the Protestant doctrine of faith. For a detailed study of mystical elements in John Calvin's theology, see Dennis E. Tamburello, *Union with Christ: John Calvin and the Mysticism of St. Bernard* (Louisville: Westminster/John Knox Press, 1994).

4. William Morris, ed., *The American Heritage Dictionary*, 1975 edition (New York: American Heritage Publishing Co.).

5. This book will only deal with Christian understandings of mysticism, but it is important to realize that mysti-

cism is a phenomenon that is common to all world religions, though it is manifested in various ways and in different degrees. For example, in Judaism there is the Kabbalah, and in Islam the Sufi movement. One of the most debated questions in the twentieth century has been whether the mystical experiences of different religions are really just variations of one common experience of the sacred. This is probably a question that is impossible to answer.

6. Bernard McGinn, "Love, Knowledge, and Mystical Union in Western Christianity: Twelfth to Sixteenth Centuries," *Church History* 56 (March 1987):7.

7. Underwood, *Mysticism*, p. 72.

8. Ernst Troeltsch, *The Social Teachings of the Christian Churches*, trans. Olive Wyon, 2 vols. (New York: Macmillan, 1931), 2:730.

9. Karl Rahner, "Mystical Experience and Mystical Theology," in *Theological Investigations*, Volume 17: *Jesus, Man, and the Church*, trans. Margaret Kohl (New York: Crossroad, 1981), pp. 90–99.

10. Ibid., p. 98. Rahner tends to connect this kind of mystical experience with what has traditionally been called a "suspension of the faculties," i.e., of memory, understanding, and will (see p. 97). In other words, we have an experience of moving beyond our normal physical and mental functions.

11. Ibid., p. 98.

12. This, incidentally, is the category in which the author finds himself.

13. Friedrich von Hügel, *The Mystical Element of Religion as Studied in St. Catherine of Genoa and Her Friends*, 2nd ed., 2 vols. (London: J. M. Dent and Sons, Ltd., 1923), 1:51–53.

14. Ibid., 1:71.

15. It might seem strange to see "biblical fundamentalists" included among those who are fixated on the institu-

tional aspect of religion. It is certainly true that many biblical fundamentalists see themselves as opponents of "institutional religion"; yet, in my experience, these people often give evidence of operating from an institutional mentality—the very thing they claim to abhor—as in the uncritical deference that people give to the pastor in some fundamentalist churches. Incidentally, this book understands "fundamentalism" in the sense defined by James Barr: "Fundamentalism begins when people begin to say that the doctrinal and practical authority of scripture is necessarily tied to its infallibility and in particular its historical inerrancy, when they maintain that its doctrinal and practical authority will stand up *only* if it is in general without error, and this means in particular only if it is without error in its apparently historical remarks." James Barr, *The Scope and Authority of the Bible* (Philadelphia: Westminster Press, 1980), p. 65. In the same essay, Barr argues that fundamentalism's function is to "create a space within which a particular religious tradition, with its doctrines, its emotions, and its traditional interpretations of scripture, along with its traditional language, habits and social organization, may continue unchanged and in strength" (p. 70). Notice how all of this has to do with buttressing *institutional* religion.

16. Of course, Christians believe that there is a "divine" element in the church, which is usually correlated with the Holy Spirit. But there is also a human element, and that element is subject to sin and error. This does not just apply to individual Christians, but to the church as a whole.

17. See the excellent study by Robert Bellah et al., *Habits of the Heart: Individualism and Commitment in American Life* (New York: Harper and Row, 1985).

18. I belong to a national organization of religion scholars that has an annual meeting attended by several thou-

sand people. Ironically, nowhere in the program booklet is there even so much as a mention of where one can *find* a worship service. It is almost as if the organization is embarrassed by religious commitment, yet it is probable that a large number of the attendees are in fact active participants in a religious community.

19. Francis of Assisi, Admonition 6, in *Francis and Clare: The Complete Works*, edited and translated by Regis Armstrong and Ignatius Brady, The Classics of Western Spirituality (New York: Paulist Press, 1982), p. 29.

20. Ibid., Admonition 7, p. 30.

21. Ironically, the book of Revelation, the book to which biblical fundamentalists frequently turn to buttress their arguments, was one of them.

22. Von Hügel, *Mystical Element of Religion*, pp. 73–75.

23. See note 11 above.

24. For example, in his introduction to *Christian Spirituality: Origins to the Twelfth Century*, Volume 16 of *World Spirituality: An Encyclopedic History of the Religious Quest* (New York: Crossroad, 1985), Bernard McGinn offers the following tentative definition of Christian spirituality: "Christian spirituality is the lived experience of Christian belief in both its general and more specialized forms....It is possible to distinguish spirituality from doctrine in that it concentrates not on faith itself, but on the reaction that faith arouses in religious consciousness and practice" (pp. xv–xvi).

25. Von Hügel, *Mystical Element of Religion*, 1:53, 65–66.

26. Ibid., 1:66, 70.

27. Ibid., 2:283.

28. See above, p. 9.

29. Von Hügel, *Mystical Element of Religion*, 2:282–83.

30. Rufus M. Jones, *Studies in Mystical Religion* (London: Macmillan, 1923), p. xv. Emphasis added.

31. Jerald C. Brauer, "Francis Rous, Puritan Mystic, 1579–1659: An Introduction to the Study of the Mystical Element in Puritanism" (Ph.D. Dissertation, University of Chicago, 1948), p. 5.

32. Perhaps the most famous of these is Meister Eckhart, whose ideas we will be dealing with later in the book. However, many other mystics were at one point or another investigated for heresy, including such great figures as Ignatius Loyola and Teresa of Avila.

33. David Tracy, in *The Analogical Imagination* (New York: Crossroad, 1981), comments on this kind of experience. He speaks of encounters with "religious classics," which he understands as texts, events, images, rituals, symbols and persons that put us in touch with the ground of reality. In Tracy's words: "What we mean in naming certain texts, events, images, rituals, symbols, and persons 'classics' is that here we recognize nothing less than the disclosure of a reality we cannot but name truth" (p. 108). He later speaks of the common experience of looking back on such an experience and concluding that it must have just been our imagination: "The interpreter may of course, in a later reflective, distancing moment, question that original religious experience and reinterpret it as some 'as-if' experience produced by the human imagination. But in the moment of encounter-response itself, the moment Christians call 'faith,' there is no 'imagine-reality-as-if-it-were-this-way' experience" (p. 164). Rather, the experience is of being "grasped" by ultimate reality.

34. John Baillie, *Our Knowledge of God* (New York: Charles Scribner's Sons, 1939), pp. 178, 181. The "other presences" of which Baillie speaks are the presence of God, the corporeal world, and other people (p. 181).

35. Ibid., pp. 182–89.

36. Bernard Lonergan, *Method in Theology* (New York: Herder and Herder, 1972), pp. 76–77.

37. Jean Gerson, *Selections from "A Deo exivit," "Contra curiositatem studentium" and "De mystica theologia speculativa,"* translated and edited by Steven Ozment (Leiden: E. J. Brill, 1969), pp. 64–65.

38. Some mystics did use the language of "essential" union at times, and they got into trouble for it! (Usually, though, what they said was distorted by those who condemned them.) The eastern religions are more comfortable with speaking of an "identity" between the believer and God—if God is even acknowledged as a separate being! For a good introduction to some of the issues relating to Christianity and eastern religions (specifically Buddhism) see Leo D. Lefebure, *Life Transformed: Meditations on the Christian Scriptures in Light of Buddhist Perspectives* (Chicago: ACTA Publications, 1989).

2. The Knowledge of God

1. One of the problems with learning the catechism was that we often did not understand what we were memorizing. We could repeat the words, but so could a tape recorder! But even if we presume an understanding of the intellectual content of the faith, there was still an ingredient missing: the connection with experience. This will be discussed below.

2. John Calvin, *Institutes of the Christian Religion*, edited by John McNeill, translated by Ford Lewis Battles, The Library of Christian Classics, Volumes 20 and 21 (Philadelphia: Westminster Press, 1960), 1.2.2 [Book 1, Chapter 2, Section 2: this is the accepted way of annotating references in the *Institutes*].

3. *Institutes* 1.2.1.

4. For more on this subject, see William Bouwsma's excellent essay on "The Spirituality of John Calvin," in *Christian Spirituality II: High Middle Ages and Reformation*, edited by Jill Raitt (New York: Crossroad, 1987). See also my *Union with Christ: John Calvin and the Mysticism of St. Bernard* (Louisville: Westminster John Knox Press, 1994).

5. Many people, myself included, find that referring to God exclusively as "he" or "him" is at the very least problematic (some find it even totally unacceptable). I use "him" here because Bernard uses the masculine pronoun in this and most other contexts. However, one does occasionally find in Bernard feminine imagery for God. This is an issue that will occupy our attention later in this chapter.

6. Bernard of Clairvaux, *On the Song of Songs I*, translated by Kilian Walsh, OSCO, Cistercian Fathers Series, No. 4 (Kalamazoo: Cistercian Publications, 1971), *SC* 8.5. SC is the accepted abbreviation for "Sermon on the Song of Songs"—thus, the reference here is to Sermon No. 8, section 5. Unless otherwise noted, all translations from the works of St. Bernard are taken from this series.

7. *On the Song of Songs II*, trans. Kilian Walsh, Cistercian Fathers Series, No. 7 (Kalamazoo: Cistercian Publications, 1983), *SC* 23.14.

8. *Institutes* 3.2.7.

9. *Institutes* 3.2.14.

10. *Institutes* 3.20.12, emphasis mine.

11. It is common nowadays to hear theologians distinguishing the "mystical" from the "prophetic." For an example, see David Tracy, *Dialogue with the Other* (Grand Rapids: Eerdmans, 1990), pp. 9–26. But, as Tracy points out in *The Analogical Imagination*, these two "strains" are not mutually exclusive, and in fact need to exist together (see pp. 203–05). I would also suggest that individuals can

be both mystics and prophets. Francis of Assisi comes most readily to mind.

12. See Bernard McGinn, "Love, Knowledge, and Mystical Union in Western Christianity: Twelfth to Sixteenth Centuries," *Church History* 56 (March 1987), p. 9.

13. Interested readers might begin by looking at one of the following books: Anne Carr's *Transforming Grace: Christian Tradition and Women's Experience* (San Francisco: Harper and Row, 1988) or Patricia Wilson-Kastner's *Faith, Feminism, and the Christ* (Philadelphia: Fortress Press, 1983).

14. Ritamary Bradley presents a long list in her article "Julian of Norwich: Writer and Mystic" in Paul Szarmach, *An Introduction to the Medieval Mystics of Europe* (Albany: SUNY Press, 1986), pp. 209–210. The list includes Irenaeus, Justin Martyr, Clement of Alexandria, John Chrysostom, Jerome, Ambrose, Augustine, Peter Lombard, Anselm, Bernard of Clairvaux, Albert the Great, Bonaventure, and even Thomas Aquinas.

15. Julian of Norwich, *Showings*, The Classics of Western Spirituality (New York: Paulist Press, 1978), p. 285. Note that there are actually two versions of the text, a shorter version that she wrote around 1373, the year of the visions, and a longer version that appeared about twenty years later. The second version adds the insights she gained from the years of further reflection on the visions. All the quotations I will be using in this chapter are from the longer text. I heartily recommend this volume as well as all the other volumes in the Paulist series.

16. In Chapter 58 of the longer text of *Showings*, she states: "In our almighty Father we have our protection and our bliss, as regards our natural substance, which is ours by creation from without beginning; and in the second person, in knowledge and wisdom we have our perfection, as regards our sensuality, our restoration, and our salvation,

for he is our Mother, brother, and saviour; and in our good Lord the Holy Spirit we have our reward and our gift for our living and our labour, endlessly surpassing all that we desire in his marvellous courtesy, out of his great plentiful grace. For all our life consists of three: In the first we have our being, and in the second we have our increasing, and in the third we have our fulfillment." *Showings*, pp. 293–94.

17. Ibid., p. 294.

18. Here Julian refers back to one of the earlier "showings," described in Chapter 4 of the longer version of the text (p. 182 in the Paulist volume).

19. *Showings*, Chapter 60, p. 297.

20. National Council of Churches of Christ in the United States, *An Inclusive Language Lectionary*, revised edition. Westminster/John Knox Press.

21. An excellent book on images of God today is Sallie McFague's *Models of God* (Philadelphia: Fortress Press, 1987). She experiments with images of God as Mother, Lover, and Friend.

22. This whole section on images of God is sure to be seen as inadequate by theological feminists, and I would agree with them. There is so much more that needs to be said, which is beyond the scope of this book: the very terms "masculine" and "feminine," for example, represent cultural stereotypes more than objective realities. The literature on this topic is vast. A few suggested readings are: for historical perspective on women and Christianity, Barbara MacHaffie, *Her Story: Women in Christian Tradition* (Philadelphia: Fortress Press, 1986); for the question of language, Mary Daly, *Beyond God the Father: Toward a Philosophy of Women's Liberation* (Boston: Beacon Press, 1973), and Rosemary Radford Ruether, *Sexism and God-Talk: Toward a Feminist Theology* (Boston: Beacon Press, 1983).

23. See Edmund Colledge's Introduction in *Meister Eckhart: The Essential Sermons, Commentaries, Treatises, and Defense*, ed. and trans. Edmund Colledge and Bernard McGinn, The Classics of Western Spirituality (New York: Paulist Press, 1981), p. 6.

24. One of the more famous of Eckhart's statements on this subject can be found in German sermon 2 on Luke 10:38. See *Meister Eckhart: The Essential Sermons, Commentaries, Treatises, and Defense*, pp. 177–81.

25. *Meister Eckhart: Teacher and Preacher*, edited by Bernard McGinn, The Classics of Western Spirituality (New York: Paulist Press, 1986), p. 63. The reference to the *Fountain of Life* is to a work by Ibn Gabirol, a Jewish medieval philosopher.

26. *Meister Eckhart: The Essential Sermons, Commentaries, Treatises, and Defense*, p. 207.

27. Colledge's Introduction in *Meister Eckhart: The Essential Sermons, Commentaries, Treatises, and Defense*, p. 13. See pp. 9–15 for an extended discussion of the condemnation of Eckhart's ideas.

28. The mystics' views on the nature of God have often been cited in the argument that there is an "alternative tradition" that is more inclusive of women and the feminine than the dominant patriarchal tradition in Christianity. This "inclusive" tradition begins in the New Testament and has manifested itself throughout Christian history, despite attempts to suppress it. See Anne E. Carr, *Transforming Grace: Christian Tradition and Women's Experience* (San Francisco: Harper and Row, 1988), pp. 46–49. Most arguments for the ordination of women combine this historical argument with a theological and ethical one (ibid., pp. 49–59). The Catholic hierarchy, of course, continues to oppose the ordination of women; but to many, it has not argued its case convincingly.

3. Grace and Freedom

1. Interested readers might consult the following sources: the article on grace in the *New Catholic Encyclopedia*, and Henri Rondet, *The Grace of Christ* (Westminster: Newman Press, 1966).

2. See Chapter 1, p. 10. This is the understanding promoted by theologians like Karl Rahner. See his *Foundations of Christian Faith: An Introduction to the Idea of Christianity*, trans. William Dych (New York: Crossroad, 1978), pp. 116–37.

3. In the last chapter, I argued for an expansion of our vocabulary in talking about God. In this chapter, I wish to follow through on this by referring to God both as "he" and "she." This may be uncomfortable for some readers; indeed, I am embarrassed to say that it still makes me uncomfortable too. But it's time to start putting our money where our mouth is!

4. See Calvin's Commentary on John 1:5, in *Calvin's New Testament Commentaries*, Vol. 4, trans. T.H.L. Parker (Grand Rapids: Eerdmans, 1961), p. 12, and *Institutes* 2.8.

5. I refer especially to the traditional debate between "justification by faith" or "by works" which came to a boiling point during the sixteenth century reformation. This is a very complicated subject, which I don't think it is necessary to develop at length here. Although there are still times when one hears people arguing about our being saved by "faith" or by our own "works," well-informed Christians today generally recognize that this way of formulating the issue of our relationship with God is oversimplified, and possibly based on a misreading of scripture. A classic study on the scriptural question is Krister Stendahl's *Paul among Jews and Gentiles* (Philadelphia: Fortress Press, 1976). It should be required reading for any-

one who would still insist on dividing Roman Catholic and Protestant views along these lines. In any case, the insistence that salvation comes from God alone was, in fact, solidly defined in church teaching long before the time of Luther. Admittedly, that teaching had been corrupted both in the intellectual life and the practice of the late medieval church. The basic point here is that responding to God's call is clearly enjoined upon us by the scriptures, even if it is understood, as we shall see, that this response is itself rooted in God's initiative.

6. Richard Kieckhefer, "The Notion of Passivity in the Sermons of John Tauler," *Recherches de Théologie Ancienne et Médiévale* 48 (1981):198. Pelagius was a monk who precipitated a major controversy around the year 400 when he suggested that human beings can become holy by their own efforts.

7. Bernard of Clairvaux, *Treatises III: On Grace and Free Choice; In Praise of the New Knighthood,* trans. Daniel O'Donovan and Conrad Greenia, Cistercian Fathers Series, No. 19 (Kalamazoo: Cistercian Publications, 1977), pp. 105–06.

8. Ibid., p. 106.

9. Bernard of Clairvaux, *Treatises II: The Steps of Humility and Pride; On Loving God,* trans. M. Ambrose Conway, OSCO and Robert Walton, OSB, Cistercian Fathers Series, No. 13 (Kalamazoo: Cistercian Publications, 1980), pp. 96–97. This statement by Bernard recalls a famous remark by Augustine, who once said that God chooses to crown as merits what in fact are his own gifts.

10. *Francis and Clare: The Complete Works,* trans. Ignatius Brady and Regis Armstrong, The Classics of Western Spirituality (New York: Paulist Press, 1982), p. 38.

11. The Rule of 1223, Chapter 1. *Francis and Clare,* p. 137.

12. Rule of 1223, Chapter 5. *Francis and Clare*, p. 140.

13. See Genesis 3:17–19, where God says to Adam: "Cursed is the ground because of you; in toil you shall eat of it all the days of your life; thorns and thistles it shall bring forth for you; and you shall eat the plants of the field. By the sweat of your face you shall eat bread until you return to the ground, for out of it you were taken; you are dust, and to dust you shall return."

14. John Tauler, *Spiritual Conferences*, trans. and edited by Eric Colledge and Sr. M. Jane, OP (Rockford: Tan Books and Publishers, 1978), p. 49 (Sermon 7 for Septuagesima); see also Sermon 2 for the Eve of the Epiphany, p. 35.

15. Ibid., Sermon 25 for Pentecost, p. 179.

16. Ibid., Sermon 25 for Pentecost, p. 185. Another example is found in Sermon 37 for the Third Sunday after Trinity, p. 76.

17. Ibid., Sermon 2 for the Eve of the Epiphany, pp. 33–34.

18. Ibid., Sermon 3 for Epiphany, p. 83.

19. Kieckhefer, "The Notion of Passivity in the Sermons of John Tauler," p. 203.

20. "Bypassing the Surgeon," in *Newsweek International*, May 11, 1992, p. 58.

21. There is a genre of literature called "apocalyptic," represented in the bible by such books as Daniel and Revelation, that *does* speak of God's "breaking into" history and inaugurating a new future. In the process, the world as we know it will "pass away." I am not in agreement with those who see these books as providing either a literal blueprint or a general outline of what is going to happen historically in the future. (Believe me, I'd be happy to be proven wrong—I'd love to see God step in and straighten things out!) This literature expresses in metaphorical lan-

guage the belief that, ultimately, good will triumph over evil. Its function at the time it was written was to give people hope and courage in the midst of persecution. (Both Daniel and Revelation were written in this kind of a context.) In fact, apocalyptic could be seen as "resistance literature." For an excellent essay on this topic, see A. A. DiLella's "The Book of Daniel Today," in *Daniel*, The Anchor Bible, trans. and ed. Louis F. Hartman, C.SS.R. and Alexander A. DiLella, OFM (New York: Doubleday, 1978), pp. 103–10. In any case, the apocalyptic sections of the bible are some of the most misunderstood and misused texts in the history of Christianity.

22. Indeed, the idea that Christianity has always been the same, and always will be the same, "now and forever, world without end, Amen!" is really an illusion—an illusion that unfortunately has been officially fostered by many Christian communities. A careful look at the history of Christian thought and practice is enough to dispel this notion. Christians did *not* think or act in the middle ages in the same way that they thought and acted in the first century, nor should Christians today think that they have to think or act now in the same way Christians did even fifty years ago. Christian history, like an individual's Christian life, is a process with many ups and downs. This topic will command our attention in the next chapter.

23. Julian of Norwich, *Showings*, Thirteenth Revelation, Chapters 27–32, pp. 224–33.

24. The conversation between God and Job (where Job does more listening than talking) continues to chapter 42.

25. For more on the problem of evil and innocent suffering, see the book by Rabbi H. Kushner, *When Bad Things Happen to Good People* (New York: Schocken Books, 1981). His response to the problem of evil, like all others that I have encountered, is not going to please everyone.

An excellent essay on this subject is "The Mystery of Suffering and Evil" by Thomas L. Sheridan, S.J., in *Living Faith: An Introduction to Theology*, by Eileen Flynn and Gloria Thomas (New York: Sheed and Ward), pp. 412–28.

26. See Thomas Aquinas; see also Rahner, *Foundations of Christian Faith*, pp. 86–89.

27. See Karl Rahner's discussion of miracles in *Foundations of Christian Faith*, pp. 257ff.

28. The story of Adam and Eve is relevant in this connection. God recognizes that they have been "tricked" by the serpent; nevertheless, he holds them responsible for the decision they made to eat the forbidden fruit.

4. Conversion: A Lifelong Process

1. *Bonaventure: The Soul's Journey into God; The Tree of Life; The Life of St. Francis*, translated by Ewert Cousins, The Classics of Western Spirituality (New York: Paulist Press, 1978), p. 315.

2. M. Scott Peck, M.D., *People of the Lie: The Hope for Healing Human Evil* (New York: Simon and Schuster, 1983). See especially Chapter 2, pp. 36–84.

3. *Francis and Clare*, p. 27.

4. *The Theologia Germanica of Martin Luther*, trans. Bengt Hoffman, The Classics of Western Spirituality (New York: Paulist Press, 1980), Ch. 12, p. 75. See the Introduction, pp. 6–12, for a discussion of the Friends of God tradition with which Tauler appears to have been associated.

5. Ibid., Ch. 3, p. 62.

6. Ibid., Ch. 10, p. 72. I should point out that some feminist writers have criticized this notion of sin as self-will and self-assertion. They claim that for many women, the problem has been the opposite: submitting to an oppressive, patriarchal culture, and *not* asserting their rights and

autonomy when they should have. See, for example, Valerie Saiving, "The Human Situation: A Feminine View," in *Womanspirit Rising: A Feminist Reader in Religion*, ed. Carol Christ and Judith Plaskow (San Francisco: Harper and Row, 1979), pp. 25–35. While I am in agreement with this critique, I do not think it invalidates the basic insight of the medieval mystics. There is a kind of self-assertion that upholds human dignity, and another kind that is narcissistic. It seems to me that all human beings, men and women alike, are capable of both.

7. Ibid., Ch. 13, p. 76.

8. Bernard of Clairvaux, "On Loving God," 1.1, *Treatises II*, p. 94.

9. See Chapter 3, pp. 47–48.

10. *On Loving God* 6.16, p. 109.

11. *On Loving God* 8.23, p. 115. Bernard is speaking here of a human nature that has been weakened by the sin of Adam and Eve.

12. *On Loving God* 8.23, p. 116.

13. *On Loving God* 8.24–25, pp. 116–117. Bernard thinks that it is self-evident that God created the world, sustains it in existence, and is the source of all good. He says in this section that "no rational creature may ignore this fact concerning itself [i.e., its status as creature in relation to God]." In our own day, there appear to be lots of rational creatures ignoring this fact, if not outrightly denying the existence of God. Thus, Bernard's argument here presupposes faith.

14. A powerful scriptural witness to this point can be found in the Magnificat (Luke 1:47–55). There Mary prays:

> He has brought down the powerful from their thrones,
> and lifted up the lowly;
> he has filled the hungry with good things,
> and sent the rich away empty.

Donal Dorr comments on this passage as follows: "Mary's theological reflection makes no concession at all to those who would like to imagine that the oppressed can be set free without disturbing those who hold power and without dismantling the structures of oppression." *Spirituality and Justice* (Maryknoll: Orbis Books, 1984), p. 39 (see pp. 36–40 for the full discussion).

15. *On Loving God* 9.26, pp. 117–18.

16. Aristotle, *The Nichomachean Ethics*, trans. David Ross revised by J. L. Ackrill and J. O. Urmson (Oxford: Oxford University Press, 1980), pp. 195–96. I am indebted to Dr. Richard Gaffney of the Philosophy Department at Siena College for sharing with me this aspect of Aristotle's wisdom.

17. *On Loving God* 9.26, p. 118.

18. Ibid.

19. Martin Luther, "The Freedom of a Christian," in *Martin Luther: Selections from His Writings*, ed. John Dillenberger (Garden City: Doubleday Anchor Books, 1961), pp. 73–74.

20. *On Loving God* 15.39, p. 131.

21. *On Loving God* 10.29, p. 121. He also comments on this in 10.27 (p. 119): "I would say that man is blessed and holy to whom it is given to experience something of this sort, so rare in life, even if it be but once and for the space of a moment."

22. See especially Sermons 23.15, 32.2, and especially 74.5–6, where Bernard speaks at some length of his own experience of ecstasy.

23. *Theologia Germanica*, Ch. 14, p. 80.

24. *Theologia Germanica*, Ch. 10, p. 71.

25. *On Loving God* 10.28, p. 120.

26. *On Loving God* 10.27, p. 119.

27. *On Loving God* 11.31, p. 122. Modern theologians

tend to speak of human beings more as "embodied spirits," and avoid the language of body-soul separation. Rahner, for example, would argue that human beings are "Spirits in the World," and after death they *remain* such, but that they are "transposed into another mode of existence." Rahner, *Foundations of Christian Faith*, p. 436. See pp. 435–441 for a more complete discussion of this topic.

28. See Rahner, *Foundations of Christian Faith*, Ch. 2, pp. 44–89.

29. See the Canticle of the Creatures in *Francis and Clare*, pp. 38–39.

30. Julian of Norwich, *Showings* (long text), Ch. 72, p. 320.

31. Perhaps the most famous is the purgative-illuminative-unitive. For a brief discussion of these stages, see Evelyn Underhill, "The Essentials of Mysticism," in *Understanding Mysticism*, ed. Richard Woods, O.P. (Garden City: Doubleday Image Books, 1980), pp. 30–41.

32. See Bernard of Clairvaux, *The Letters of Bernard of Clairvaux*, trans. Bruno Scott James (Chicago: Henry Regnery Co., 1953), Letter 91 (to the Abbots assembled at Soissons), p. 141. The letter is listed as No. 94 in this translation.

33. M. Scott Peck, M.D., *The Road Less Traveled: A New Psychology of Love, Traditional Values and Spiritual Growth* (New York: Simon and Schuster, 1978), p. 15.

34. One might think of cigarette ads, for example, that show young and healthy people enjoying a smoke. The surgeon general's warning somehow gets lost behind the slick image.

35. See *John of the Cross: Selected Writings*, ed. Kieran Kavanaugh, O.C.D., The Classics of Western Spirituality (New York: Paulist Press, 1987), pp. 157–61 (editor's introduction) and pp. 162–209 (selections from the text).

36. These remarks are dedicated to the late Rev. Kenneth Walsh, whose joy and warmth inspired me as a friar.

5. Contemplation and Action

1. Evelyn Underhill, *Mysticism*, pp. 328, 330, 333.

2. SC 46.2.

3. Marie-Bernard Saïd, O.S.B., in his Introduction to Bernard of Clairvaux, *Sermons on Conversion*, trans. Saïd, Cistercian Fathers Series, No. 25 (Kalamazoo: Cistercian Publications, 1981), p. 20.

4. *SC* 62.6.

5. In *SC* 84.7, Bernard says: "Let those who do not have such an experience believe, so that by the merit of their faith they will reap the fruit of experience." (My translation)

6. *SC* 50.5–6.

7. *SC* 50.6 and 47.4.

8. See *SC* 57.9. Recall, too, what Bernard said when he discussed the third stage of loving God. At this stage, when we begin to love God for God's sake, our love becomes pure. As a result, we will no longer have trouble "fulfilling the commandment to love [our] neighbor" (*On Loving God* 9:26, p. 118).

9. *Meister Eckhart: Teacher and Preacher*, ed. Bernard McGinn (with the collaboration of Frank Tobin and Elvira Borgstadt), The Classics of Western Spirituality (New York: Paulist Press, 1986), pp. 338–39.

10. Ibid., p. 339.

11. Ibid., p. 342.

12. Ibid., p. 343.

13. Ibid., p. 344.

14. For a more complete exposition of this aspect of

Eckhart's thought, see Richard Kieckhefer, "Meister Eckhart's Conception of Union with God," *Harvard Theological Review* 71 (1978):203–25.

15. This biographical information is summarized from the Introduction by Kieran Kavanaugh in *Teresa of Avila: The Interior Castle*, trans. Kieran Kavanaugh and Otilio Rodriguez, The Classics of Western Spirituality (New York: Paulist Press, 1979), pp. 1ff. My quotations of the work are also from this volume.

16. The works of John of the Cross are also relevant in this regard, especially his *Dark Night of the Soul*.

17. In 1562, Teresa wrote her Autobiography (*The Book of Her Life*), largely to try to explain herself to her directors and confessors.

18. *The Interior Castle* 1.2.17, p. 47.

19. Ibid., 4.1.7, p. 70.

20. Ibid., 1.1.8, pp. 38–39.

21. Ibid., 2.1.3, p. 49.

22. Ibid., 3.1.5, p. 57.

23. Ibid., 3.1.8, p. 59.

24. Ibid., 3.2.12, p. 65.

25. Ibid., 4.1.1–2, pp. 67–68.

26. Ibid., 4.1.4, pp. 68–69.

27. As mentioned earlier, this is one of the classic Protestant criticisms of mysticism. It would certainly not apply to Teresa.

28. *The Interior Castle* 4.2.3–4, p. 74.

29. *The Interior Castle* 4.2.9, pp. 76–77.

30. *The Interior Castle* 7.1.5, pp. 174–75.

31. Teresa describes union with God in this dwelling place as a kind of "intellectual" vision of the Trinity. See *The Interior Castle* 7.1.6, p. 175. Eckhart's mysticism has been described as more "intellectual" than "affective," as we shall see in the next chapter.

32. *The Interior Castle* 7.3.2,8, pp. 183–84.

33. *The Interior Castle* 7.4.6, pp. 189–90. Emphasis added.

34. *The Interior Castle* 7.4.9, p. 191.

35. *The Interior Castle* 7.4.12, p. 192. In the following section (13, pp. 192–93), Teresa puts her own twist on the Martha and Mary story. To the objection that Jesus said that Mary had chosen the better part, Teresa responds: "The answer is that she had already performed the task of Martha, pleasing the Lord by washing His feet and drying them with her hair." This is a reference to Luke 7:37–38. (But is this the same Mary? Contemporary commentators would say no.) Notice that Teresa's interpretation here is the opposite of Eckhart's, and is indeed the more conventional one: that Mary has "moved beyond" a purely "active" spirituality. But her point is that we need both.

36. *The Interior Castle* 7.4.14, p. 193.

37. Groups like Bread for the World and Amnesty International come to mind here.

38. *The Interior Castle* 7.4.15, p. 194.

39. John Tauler, *Spiritual Conferences*, trans. and ed. E. Colledge and Sr. M. Jane, O.P. (Rockford: Tan Books and Publishers, 1978), Sermon 8 for the First Friday in Lent, p. 53.

40. See Karl Rahner, "Reflections on the Unity of the Love of Neighbor and the Love of God," in *Theological Investigations*, Volume 6, translated by Karl H. and Boniface Kruger (Baltimore: Helicon Press, 1969), pp. 231–49.

6. Union with God

1. Bernard of Clairvaux, *On Loving God* 10.28, *Treatises II*, p. 120.

2. Etienne Gilson, *La théologie mystique de Saint Bernard*, pp. 144–45. Translation mine.

3. Jean Gerson, *Selections*, pp. 64–65. See Chapter 1, note 34.

4. *On the Song of Songs IV*, trans. Irene Edmonds, Cistercian Fathers Series, No. 40 (Kalamazoo: Cistercian Publications, 1980), Sermon 83.3, p. 182.

5. See Chapter 2.

6. See *The Interior Castle* 6.4ff for details.

7. Ibid., 7.1.5, p. 174.

8. *The Interior Castle* 7.2.3, p. 178.

9. Ibid., 7.2.7, p. 180.

10. Ibid., 7.3.11, p. 186.

11. Ibid., 7.2.9, p. 181.

12. Ibid., 7.3.10, p. 185.

13. Ibid., 7.2.5, p. 179.

14. Albrecht Ritschl, *The Christian Doctrine of Justification and Reconciliation*, Volume 3, translation edited by H. R. Mackintosh and A. B. Macaulay (New York: Scribner, 1900), pp. 593–94.

15. An excellent example is found in Sermon 52.2 on the Song, *On the Song of Songs III*, trans. Kilian Walsh and Irene Edmonds, Cistercian Fathers Series No. 31 (Kalamazoo: Cistercian Publications, 1979), pp. 50–51.

16. See especially *On the Song of Songs IV*, Sermon 67.8, p. 12, and Sermon 68.1, p. 17.

17. Ibid., *IV*, Sermon 83.6, p. 186. Emphasis added.

18. *Institutes* 3.11.10.

19. Many readers may be aware that Calvin expressly taught a doctrine of "double predestination": that is, specific people are predestined to glory and others to eternal damnation. Many theologians today, including some in the Reformed tradition, would say that Calvin was mistaken in this belief, which he felt bound to maintain from his

understanding of the scriptures and of human experience. Readers who are interested in pursuing this matter further might wish to consult Timothy George's book, *Theology of the Reformers* (Nashville: Broadman Press, 1988).

20. *Institutes* 3.2.25.

21. See *Institutes* 3.1.3.

22. *Institutes* 3.2.24.

23. John Calvin's Commentary on Ephesians 5:31, *Calvin's New Testament Commentaries*, Vol. 11, *The Epistles of Paul the Apostle to the Galatians, Ephesians, Philippians, and Colossians*, translated by T. H. L. Parker (Grand Rapids: Eerdmans, 1965), p. 209. Emphasis added.

24. Letter to Peter Martyr, 8 August 1555, translation mine. This document is found in Vol. 15 of Calvin's works in the *Corpus Reformatorum*, edited by W. Baum, E. Cunitz, and E. Reutz.

25. Letter to Peter Martyr, 8 August 1555.

26. *Institutes* 2.8.51.

27. See Chapter 5, pp. 83–85.

28. *Institutes* 2.8.54.

29. *Institutes* 3.19.22.

30. Some of the following is adapted from my article "Bernard of Clairvaux in the Thought of Meister Eckhart," *Cistercian Studies Quarterly* 28.1 (1993), especially pp. 82–88.

31. *Essential Eckhart*, pp. 259–60.

32. *Essential Eckhart*, p. 270.

33. *Essential Eckhart*, p. 272.

34. See, for example, *On the Song of Songs II*, trans. Kilian Walsh, Cistercian Fathers Series, No. 7 (Kalamazoo: Cistercian Publications, 1983), Sermon 31.6, p. 129.

35. See *On Loving God* 10.28 for a reference to this and other images, e.g., molten iron becoming like fire, and air on a sunny day being transformed into sunshine.

36. German Sermon 22 in *Essential Eckhart*, p. 196.

37. Bernard McGinn, "Theological Summary," in *Essential Eckhart*, p. 56.

38. Bernard McGinn, "Love, Knowledge, and Mystical Union," p. 16.

39. *Essential Eckhart*, p. 187.

40. *Essential Eckhart*, p. 188.

41. *Essential Eckhart*, p. 207.

42. See Chapter 1, p. 22.

43. See Chapter 1, p. 21.

44. "Theological Summary," *Essential Eckhart*, p. 56. In addition to the McGinn articles already cited, see John D. Caputo, "Fundamental Themes in Meister Eckhart's Mysticism," *The Thomist* 42 (1978):197–225, and Richard Kieckhefer, "Meister Eckhart's Conception of Union with God," *Harvard Theological Review* 71 (1978):203–25.

45. See Edmund Colledge in *Essential Eckhart*, p. 13. Interested readers are encouraged to read the historical and theological introductions in this volume in their entirety.

46. *Essential Eckhart*, "Commentaries on Genesis" 14, p. 87.

47. John D. Caputo, "Fundamental Themes in Meister Eckhart's Mysticism," pp. 220–21.

48. Richard Kieckhefer calls this a "habitual" and "non-abstractive" union with God. By "habitual" he means a "habitual consciousness of God's presence which persists as one carries out one's ordinary activities," as opposed to "a sudden and ecstatic irruption upon one's life, which occurs briefly and intermittently." By "non-abstractive" he means a union that is "compatible with...ordinary consciousness," rather than a union that "precludes consciousness of the spatio-temporal world." Kieckhefer, "Meister Eckhart's Conception of Union with God," pp. 203–04.

49. John Tauler, Sermon 21 for the Ascension, *Spiritual Conferences*, p. 99.

50. Tauler, Sermon 28, translated by Steven Ozment in *Homo Spiritualis*, p. 38.

51. Tauler, Sermon 11, *Spiritual Conferences*, p. 177.

52. Tauler, Sermon 37, translated by Steven Ozment in *Homo Spiritualis*, p. 43. I have taken the liberty here of translating the terms "von gnaden" and "von naturen," which Ozment leaves in German.

53. Heinrich Denifle, *Die deutschen mystiker des 14. Jahrhunderts: Beitrag zur Deutung ihrer Lehre* (Freiburg in der Schweiz: Paulusverlag, 1951), p. 166. Translation mine.

Epilogue

1. See David Tracy, *Dialogue with the Other*, pp. 9–26, and also *The Analogical Imagination*, pp. 202–18.

Glossary of Mystical Authors

The following writers are referred to frequently in the chapters of *Ordinary Mysticism*. I chose to focus on these authors mainly because they are the ones that I found most inspiring and accessible when I began my own study of Christian mysticism. There are certainly many others whose writings are equally worthy of attention but who are not included here. Several of these are mentioned in the Suggestions for Further Reading.

Bernard of Clairvaux (1090-1153) was a member of the Cistercians, a reformed Benedictine monastic community. He was well-known in his day as a theologian, a statesman, and a mystic. Bernard's mystical theology is characterized by an emphasis on a "union of love" with God, often expressed (as in his *Sermons on the Song of Songs*) using bride-bridegroom imagery. Bernard's influence can be seen in many later mystical writers, including Meister Eckhart and the Protestant reformers Martin Luther and John Calvin.

John Calvin (1509-1564) became the leader of the Protestant Reformation in Geneva, Switzerland and the first great systematizer of Protestant thought. Although he never speaks in his writings of having had any contemplative mystical experiences, his theology reflects a certain mystical sensitivity. For example, his notion of faith is strongly experiential and not just intellectual; and he believes that those who have faith are in "mystical union" with Christ, a union he most often describes with the image of "engrafting." Calvin has often been thought of as a cold dogmatician, but a close look at his works reveals him to be a profoundly spiritual writer.

Francis of Assisi (c. 1182-1226) was the son of an Italian merchant who turned from a life of a soldier and trader to that of an itinerant preacher who embraced poverty and served the poor and outcast of his day. He founded the order that bears his name (Franciscan) and inspired Clare of Assisi to found a companion order for women. Francis was singularly devoted to the Passion of Christ and desired to share in it in the most intimate way. In a mystical experience, he was granted the gift of the stigmata (the wounds of Christ in his hands, feet, and side). He was also a nature-mystic, as can be seen in his famous "Canticle of Brother Sun."

Julian of Norwich (1342-c. 1423) was an anchoress (solitary) who lived in a cell attached to the Church of St. Julian in Norwich, England. Little is known of her life, save that she became a spiritual guide to many people in her day. She experienced a series of revelations or "showings" that focused on the love of God for humanity. Particularly striking are the frequent references in the text to God as "mother." Julian's use of this language has helped contemporary Christians to expand their image of God and break away from purely patriarchal conceptions.

Meister Eckhart (c. 1260-1327) was a Dominican priest, theologian, and preacher who lived in the Rhineland region of Germany. His mystical theology sometimes spoke of an identity between God and the graced soul; for this and other reasons, some of his ideas were formally condemned by the church. However, a careful reading of

Eckhart reveals a highly nuanced system of thought that was undoubtedly misunderstood by his contemporary critics. Eckhart also promoted the idea of an inner detachment that allows us to enjoy unity with God in the context of our everyday activities, rather than through contemplation.

John Tauler (c. 1300-1361) was also a Dominican priest, theologian, and preacher. He was a disciple of Meister Eckhart (though this may have been only through Eckhart's writings and not through personal contact). His mystical theology shows many of the same characteristics as Eckhart's, but is more restrained than that of his teacher. Tauler became a spiritual director for Dominican nuns and for a spiritual movement of his time called the "Friends of God."

Teresa of Avila (1515-1582) was a Spanish Carmelite nun who became a great contemplative and a source of spiritual guidance to many of her contemporaries. In Roman Catholicism she is honored with the title "Doctor of the Church," which recognizes her as an outstanding spiritual teacher. Teresa became the founder of several Carmelite monasteries for women that were centered on prayer. In the process, she had to thrust herself into an "active" life that was often complicated and demanding. Teresa's mysticism reflects a great concern for balance between the active and contemplative dimensions of the spiritual life.

Suggestions for Further Reading

Primary Sources in Translation

Arndt, Johann. *True Christianity*. Translated by Peter C. Erb. The Classics of Western Spirituality. New York: Paulist Press, 1979. A mystic in the Lutheran tradition.

Bernard of Clairvaux: Selected Works. Translated by G. R. Evans. The Classics of Western Spirituality. New York: Paulist Press, 1987.

Bernard of Clairvaux. *On Loving God*. Translated by Robert Walton, O.S.B. With an analytical commentary by Emero Stiegman. Cistercian Fathers Series, No. 13B. Kalamazoo, MI: Cistercian Publications, 1995. A new edition of the translation cited in this book.

Bernard of Clairvaux. *Treatises III: On Grace and Free Choice; In Praise of the New Knighthood*. Translated by Daniel O'Donovan and Conrad Greenia. Cistercian Fathers Series, No. 19. Kalamazoo, MI: Cistercian Publications, 1977.

Bonaventure: The Soul's Journey into God; The Tree of Life; The Life of St. Francis. Translated by Ewert Cousins. The Classics of Western Spirituality. New York: Paulist Press, 1978. A key Franciscan mystic.

155

Calvin, John. *Institutes of the Christian Religion.* Edited by John T. McNeill. Translated by Ford Lewis Battles. Library of Christian Classics, vols. 20 and 21. Philadelphia: Westminster Press, 1960.

The Cloud of Unknowing. Edited by James Walsh, S.J. The Classics of Western Spirituality. New York: Paulist Press, 1981. An anonymous English work on contemplative union.

Dupré, Louis and James Wiseman, Editors. *Light from Light: An Anthology of Christian Mysticism.* New York: Paulist Press, 1988. A fine one-volume anthology of mystical texts.

Francis and Clare: The Complete Works. Edited and translated by Regis Armstrong and Ignatius Brady. The Classics of Western Spirituality. New York: Paulist Press, 1982.

Hadewijch: The Complete Works. Translated by Mother Columba Hart, O.S.B. The Classics of Western Spirituality. New York: Paulist Press, 1980. A thirteenth century female mystic.

Hildegard of Bingen: Scivias. Translated by Mother Columba Hart and Jane Bishop. The Classics of Western Spirituality. New York: Paulist Press, 1990. A twelfth century visionary nun.

John of the Cross: Selected Writings. Edited by Kieran Kavanaugh, O.C.D. The Classics of Western Spirituality. New York: Paulist Press, 1987.

Julian of Norwich. *Showings.* Translated by Edmund Colledge, O.S.A. and James Walsh, S.J. The Classics of Western Spirituality. New York: Paulist Press, 1978.

Meister Eckhart: The Essential Sermons, Commentaries, Treatises, and Defense. Edited and translated by Edmund Colledge and Bernard McGinn. The Classics of Western Spirituality. New York: Paulist Press, 1981.

Meister Eckhart: Teacher and Preacher. Edited by Bernard

McGinn. *The Classics of Western Spirituality*. New York: Paulist Press, 1986.

Tauler, John. *Spiritual Conferences*. Translated and edited by Eric Colledge and Sr. M. Jane, O.P. Rockford, IL: Tan Books and Publishers, 1978.

Teresa of Avila. *The Interior Castle*. Translated by Kieran Kavanaugh, O.C.D. and Otilio Rodriguez, O.C.D. The Classics of Western Spirituality. New York: Paulist Press, 1979.

The Theologia Germanica of Martin Luther. Translated by Bengt Hoffman. The Classics of Western Spirituality. New York: Paulist Press, 1980.

Selected Secondary Sources

Bynum, Carolyn Walker. *Jesus as Mother: Studies in the Spirituality of the High Middle Ages*. Berkeley: University of California Press, 1982. A fine collection of essays.

Egan, Harvey D. *What Are They Saying About Mysticism?* New York: Paulist Press, 1982. An introduction to contemporary scholarly approaches to mysticism.

Idel, Moshe and Bernard McGinn, Editors. *Mystical Union and Monotheistic Faith: An Ecumenical Dialogue*. New York: Macmillan, 1989. Contains an excellent article by Bernard McGinn on love, knowledge, and mystical union.

McGinn, Bernard. *The Foundations of Mysticism: Origins to the Fifth Century*. Volume I of *The Presence of God: A History of Western Christian Mysticism*. New York: Crossroad, 1991.

_____. *The Growth of Mysticism: Gregory the Great through the 12th Century*. Volume II of *The Presence of God: A History of Western Christian Mysticism*. New York: Crossroad, 1994.

McGinn, Bernard and John Meyendorff, Editors. *Christian Spirituality I: Origins to the Twelfth Century.* World Spirituality, Volume 16. New York: Crossroad, 1985.

Rahner, Karl. "Mystical Experience and Mystical Theology." In *Theological Investigations,* Vol. 17, pp. 90-99. Translated by Margaret Kohl. New York: Crossroad, 1981.

Raitt, Jill, Editor. *Christian Spirituality II: High Middle Ages and Reformation.* World Spirituality, Volume 17. New York: Crossroad, 1987. See especially the articles on the spirituality of the sixteenth century reformers.

Szarmach, Paul, Editor. *An Introduction to the Medieval Mystics of Europe.* Albany: State University of New York Press, 1984. Fine articles on many of the medieval mystics.

Tamburello, Dennis E. *Union with Christ: John Calvin and the Mysticism of St. Bernard.* Louisville: Westminster/John Knox Press, 1994. A comparison of the notion of mystical union in Bernard and Calvin.

Underhill, Evelyn. *Mysticism.* New York: E. P. Dutton and Co., 1961. A classic introductory text.

Von Hügel, Friedrich. *The Mystical Element of Religion as Studied in St. Catherine of Genoa and Her Friends.* Second Edition. 2 Volumes. London: J. M. Dent and Sons, 1923.

Woods, Richard, Editor. *Understanding Mysticism.* Garden City: Doubleday, 1980. A helpful collection of essays on various topics and issues related to mysticism.

Index of Scripture References

Index of Names

Index of Subjects